We·the PEOPLE

**Build Our Nation**

# Workbook for Reading and Review

# Grade 5

**Houghton Mifflin Company • Boston**

Atlanta • Dallas • Geneva, Illinois • Palo Alto • Princeton

WE·THE
PEOPLE

# Build
# Our Nation

Selection from "Colonists in Bondage: Indentured Servants in America," from *Early American Life* magazine, October 1979. Copyright © 1979 by The Early American Society, Inc. Reprinted by permission.

Developed by PiperStudiosInc.
Illustration: PiperStudiosInc
Photography: © 1996 PhotoDisc, Inc.
Maps: Maryland CartoGraphics, a division of GeoSystems Global Corporation

Printed in U.S.A.
ISBN: 0-395-89142-6

56789-HS-03 02 01 00 99 98

# Table of Contents

WE·THE PEOPLE

Build Our Nation

WE·THE PEOPLE

**Build Our Nation**

Name _____    Date _____

Comprehension Strategy: Previewing a Lesson

# Regions and People

When you **preview** a lesson, you look ahead to find out what you will learn.

**Preview Lesson 2. Read the lesson title, the Main Idea sentence, the headings, and the Focus questions. Write the headings below.**

     **page 19 (lesson title):** <u>Regions and People</u> _____

1.   **page 19 (heading):** _____

2.   **page 20 (heading):** _____

**Now look at the illustrations in Lesson 2, including the maps, the graph, and the photographs. Describe what each illustration on pages 20 and 21 shows.**

     **page 19:** <u>The map shows ways that Indiana can be divided into regions.</u>

3.   **page 20:** _____

4.   **page 21:** _____

     **pages 22-23:** <u>The map and photographs show the cultural regions in the United</u>

              <u>States.</u>

              <u>The photographs show a folk festival in Seattle and a clambake in</u>

              <u>Massachusetts.</u>

5.   **Think about the lesson title, headings, Main Idea sentence, Focus questions, illustrations, and captions. What do you think you will learn about in Lesson 2? Answer with a complete sentence.**

     _____

6.   **What part of the lesson do you most want to learn about? Answer with a complete sentence.**

     _____

Name _____ Date _____

# Regions and People

Review pages 19-23 to answer these questions. Choose the best answer. Circle the letter next to your choice.

1. **Why do geographers divide land into regions?**
   A. to make maps easier to read
   B. to make the geography of an area easier to understand
   C. to make it easier to read directions
   D. to help people understand plants and animals

2. **In which region is Florida?**
   A. South
   B. West
   C. Northeast
   D. Midwest

3. **What is an *immigrant*?**
   A. a person who comes to a new place or country to live
   B. someone who studies the earth and its features
   C. a person who moves from one region to another
   D. someone who travels to a foreign country to do religious work

4. **What is *culture*?**
   A. the right to fair and equal treatment of all people
   B. a variety of groups of people controlled by one government
   C. the language, beliefs, and customs of a group of people
   D. the things that surround someone, including land and water

5. **Which group of immigrants were brought here against their will in the colonial period?**
   A. Native Americans
   B. African Americans
   C. Hispanics
   D. Asian Americans

Lesson Review

Name _____   Date _____

## Comparing Population Maps

# People Patterns

Study these population maps to see how the West grew from 1890 to 1990.

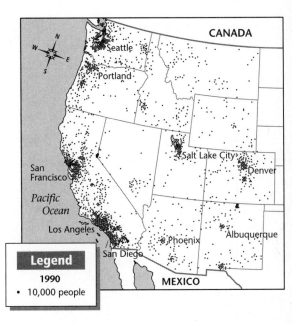

1. **List two cities that had sparse populations (few people) in 1890, but dense populations in 1990.**

   _____

2. **In 1990 Phoenix was the ninth largest city in the United States. The area around Phoenix is hot, dry desert land. Why do you think few people settled there in the 1890s, but many people live there now?**

   _____

   _____

3. **Write one difference and one similarity between the West's population in 1890 and 1990.**

   _____

   _____

Name _____ Date _____

## Comparing Population Maps

# Living in Colorado

These maps show Colorado's landforms and its 1890 and 1990 populations.

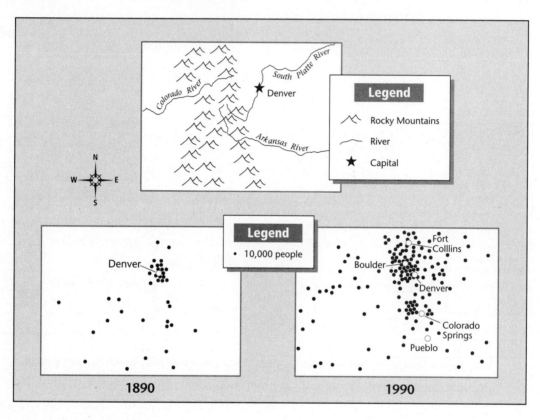

Answer the following questions.

1. **In the 1800s, many people moved to Colorado to mine gold and silver. Why do you think Denver became Colorado's largest city?**

_____

2. **Using information from all three maps, compare where people lived in 1890 to where people live in 1990. How are they alike? Different?**

_____

_____

_____

Name _____ Date _____

Vocabulary Skill: Words About a Topic

# People and the Environment

This lesson explains how the environment can affect people's lives.
The lesson also discusses ways in which people have changed
their environment. Here are some of the words used in the lesson:

| | | |
|---|---|---|
| climate | levees | adapt |
| survive | clearing | irrigate |

**Write each word under the sentence that describes it or gives clues to its meaning.**

1. People build these next to rivers to stop them from overflowing.

   _____

2. Native Americans and colonists did this to create space for homes and farms.

   _____

3. Farmers bring water to their crops by doing this to their fields.

   _____

4. This affects how people dress in summer and in winter.

   _____

5. This means "Change to meet the demands of the world around you."

   _____

6. People cannot do this if they don't adapt to their environments.

   _____

Name _____ Date _____

# People and the Environment

Review pages 26-29 to answer these questions. Choose the best answer. Circle the letter next to your choice.

1. **What is the *environment*?**
   A. a variety of territories and groups of people controlled by government
   B. the things that surround someone, including water and land
   C. a section of a city where people who share the same culture live
   D. another name for the flooding waters of the Mississippi River

2. **Which has usually happened throughout human history?**
   A. People have used adobe to build homes.
   B. The environment has shaped people and their homes.
   C. People have successfully held back heavy rains.
   D. There has been plenty of rain throughout the Southwest.

3. **How does climate influence the way we build our homes?**
   A. In the North, a steep roof lets snow slide off in winter.
   B. In the South, a porch keeps the rain off, but lets breezes in.
   C. In the Southwest, houses with thick adobe walls stay cool inside.
   D. all of the above

4. **What is *irrigation*?**
   A. the science of planning and controlling the direction of a ship
   B. a large farm where one crop is grown
   C. a method of moving water in order to grow crops in dry areas
   D. a product shipped to another country to be sold

5. **How does the environment affect where cities are built?**
   A. City roads follow the shape of the land.
   B. Towns and cities spread out according to the shape of the land.
   C. Cities are often built near natural resources.
   D. all of the above

Name _____ Date _____

*Environment and Society*

# How Have People Changed the Everglades?

Use the map below to answer the following questions. Write your answers on the map and below.

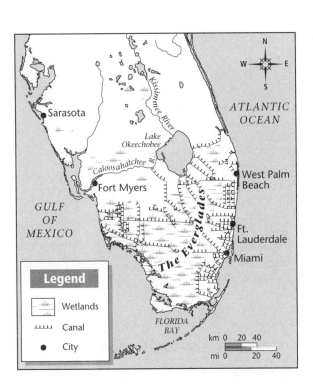

1. **Locate four major cities that are now situated near the Everglades and tell**

   **which coast they're on.** _____

   _____

2. **How many different waterways lead into or out of Lake Okeechobee?**
   **Identify the waterways.**

   _____

3. **Using only waterways, use your pencil to trace the most direct route from**
   **the Atlantic Ocean to the Gulf of Mexico.**

Think Like a Geographer                    Workbook for Reading and Review       **9**

Name _____ Date _____

# Identifying Landforms

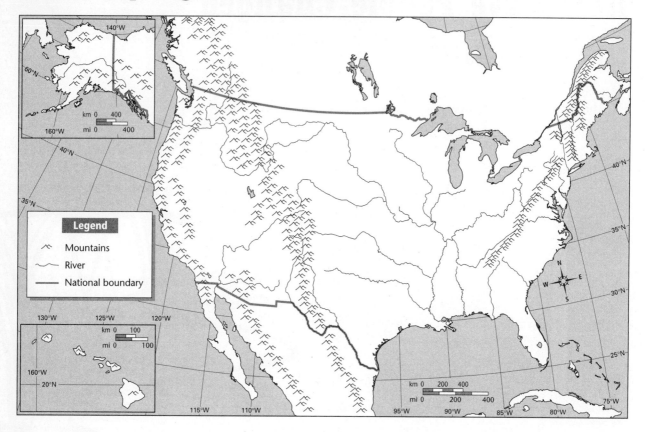

**Legend**

⌃ Mountains

⌒ River

— National boundary

Use the map above to answer the following questions.

1. Using the maps in your textbook, find and label each of the following:
   Colorado River, Grand Canyon, Death Valley, and Great Salt Lake.

2. Near which of these landforms would the most people live? Why?

_____

_____

_____

Name _____   Date _____

# The Land and the People

Review pages 12-33 to answer these questions. Choose the best answer. Circle the letter next to your choice.

1.  **What are the names and locations of the two mountain ranges that cross the U.S. from north to south?**
    A.  the Rocky Mountains in the east and the Appalachian Mountains in the west
    B.  the Teton Mountains in the west and the Allegheny Mountains in the east
    C.  the Allegheny Mountains in the west and the Teton Mountains in the east
    D.  the Rocky Mountains in the west and the Appalachian Mountains in the east

2.  **What are the United States' important natural resources?**
    A.  corn, trees, nuts, gold, and spices
    B.  rice, soybeans, flowers, and bananas
    C.  energy resources, minerals, water, and land
    D.  solar power, diamonds, olives, and grain

3.  **What is the major use of mineral resources in the United States?**
    A.  to build new kinds of transportation
    B.  to be used in energy and manufacturing
    C.  to be sold to other countries to use
    D.  to flavor food at restaurants

4.  **What are some ways geographers divide land into regions?**
    A.  by the land's location or its physical features
    B.  by the people who live there and share common characteristics
    C.  by the crops grown and the products produced there
    D.  all of the above

5.  **What is the *Breadbasket*?**
    A.  a physical region with many trees where baskets are woven
    B.  a human region where people eat mostly bread
    C.  a region with five lakes on the border between the U.S. and Canada
    D.  an economic region that is the agricultural center of the U.S.

Name _____  Date _____

6. **Why do Americans celebrate so many different holidays, such as Hanukkah and St. Patrick's Day?**

   A. People who came to the U.S. brought their native cultures with them.

   B. Americans love to have parties and laugh, talk, and enjoy meals with each other.

   C. The Native Americans began all these holidays many, many years ago.

   D. Television and movies have brought customs from all over the world to the U.S.

7. **What effect has technology had on our environment?**

   A. Humans can now change the environment in good and bad ways.

   B. There has been no change to our environment because of technology.

   C. Technology has made our environment change more slowly than it used to.

   D. Because of technology, people don't have to be concerned about the environment.

8. **How did the creation of the Hoover Dam change the environment in a positive way?**

   A. It made it difficult for fish and wildlife to live there.

   B. It used lots of concrete.

   C. It created a lake that is used to irrigate over a million acres of land.

   D. It made the Colorado River drier and shallower.

9. **What is a *reservoir*?**

   A. a lake where water is stored for future use

   B. a large area of land left in its natural condition

   C. land set aside for Native Americans

   D. all of the above

10. **Who is responsible for our country's natural resources?**

    A. only the park rangers in national parks

    B. all people who live in the United States

    C. mostly the national government

    D. people from all over the world

Name _____ Date _____

Using B.C., A.D., and Centuries

# Keeping Track of Time

This timeline includes some of the important events in B.C. and A.D. that you've learned about. Read it carefully and answer the questions below.

| 2000 B.C. | 1000 B.C. | A.D. 1 | A.D. 1000 | A.D. 2000 |
|---|---|---|---|---|

| 1000 B.C. | 400 B.C. | 150 B.C. | A.D. 700 | A.D. 900 | A.D. 1100 | A.D. 1130 | A.D. 1325 |
|---|---|---|---|---|---|---|---|
| Adena culture begins building mounds | Maya begin building pyramids | Teotihuacan established | Anasazi build pueblos on mesas | Mayan culture begins to disappear | Cahokia built | Anasazi experience decades of drought | Aztec city Tenochtitlan established |

1. **On the timeline, draw a star where B.C. ends and A.D. begins.**

2. **Look at the B.C. years.**

   a. In what year did the Maya begin building pyramids?_____

   b. In what year did the Adena begin building mounds?_____

3. **Look at the A.D. years.**

   a. What happened in A.D. 700?_____

   b. How many years ago was A.D. 700? _____

   c. What year is it today? (Use A.D.)_____

4. **Practice counting A.D. centuries.**

   a. In which century did the Anasazi experience droughts?_____

   b. In which century was Tenochtitlan established?_____

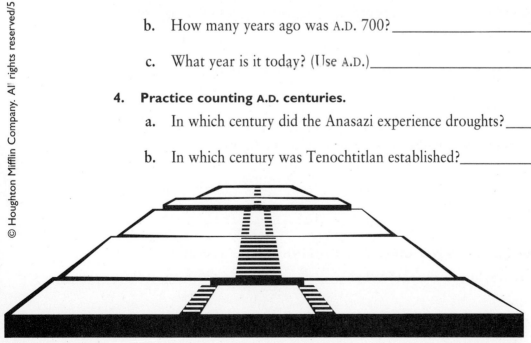

Name _____    Date _____

Using B.C., A.D., and Centuries

# When Were They Built?

Use the information in the chart to finish the timeline. Draw arrows connecting
the labels to their position on the timeline. If the data tells which A.D. century,
but not which year, place it in the center of the century. For example, if a
structure was built in the 19th century, you would place it at A.D. 1850.

| Structure | Location | Approximate Date built |
|---|---|---|
| Angkor Wat | Cambodia | A.D. 12th century |
| Cliff Palace | United States | A.D. 13th century |
| Colosseum | Italy | A.D. 80 |
| Hanging Gardens | Babylon | 600 B.C. |
| Parthenon | Greece | 440 B.C. |
| Taj Mahal | India | A.D. 1650 |
| Tikal Pyramids | Guatemala | 200 B.C. |

1000 B.C.    500 B.C.    A.D. 1    A.D. 500    A.D. 1000    A.D. 1500

Hanging      Parthenon      Tikal      Colosseum      Angkor      Cliff      Taj
Gardens                     Pyramids                   Wat        Palace     Mahal

1. **Egyptians began building their pyramids about 2600 B.C. How would you
   need to change this timeline to be able to place the Egyptian Pyramids on it?**

   _____

   _____

2. **If you could choose a year other than the birth of Jesus as year one,
   which year would you choose? Why?** _____

   _____

Name _____ Date _____

Comprehension Skill: Making Generalizations

# Life in Eastern Woodlands

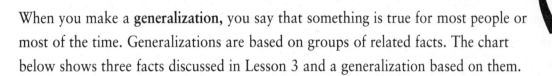

When you make a **generalization,** you say that something is true for most people or most of the time. Generalizations are based on groups of related facts. The chart below shows three facts discussed in Lesson 3 and a generalization based on them.

**Fact:** Native American groups in the Eastern Woodlands lived in dense forests.

**Fact:** All of these groups used wood and bark as building materials.

**Fact:** All of these groups hunted animals that lived in the forests.

**Generalization:** Native American groups in the Eastern Woodlands had much in common.

1.  **The chart below shows three facts from Lesson 3. Circle the generalization that can be made about these facts.**

**Fact:** Northern Native American groups built homes with thick walls to keep out the cold.

**Fact:** The Calusas of Florida took much of their food from the sea.

**Fact:** Native Americans who lived in forests hunted deer to eat.

**Generalization:**

    A.   Religion was an important part of Native Americans' lives.

    B.   Native Americans' everyday lives were shaped by their environments.

    C.   The foods that Native Americans ate depended on their environment.

2.  **Using facts from Lesson 3, write a generalization about Creek villages.**

**Fact:** In Creek villages, buildings for council meetings surrounded the central plaza.

**Fact:** Creek ceremonies took place in a central plaza.

**Fact:** Creek people built their homes around the plaza.

**Generalization:** _____

_____

Name _____ Date _____

# Life in Eastern Woodlands

Review pages 52-55 to answer these questions. Choose the best answer. Circle the letter next to your choice.

1. **What are the *woodlands*?**

   A. the unsettled land found in Eastern Europe

   B. groups of homes built in the woods by early settlers

   C. the forested eastern half of North America

   D. places where only wild animals can survive the harsh winters

2. **Which Native American group were NOT Woodlands Indians?**

   A. the Iroquois

   B. the Mohawks

   C. the Creek

   D. the Anasazi

3. **What did Woodlands Indians use to build their homes?**

   A. sand and mud

   B. wood and bark

   C. bricks and stones

   D. leaves and moss

4. **How did the environment shape what the Woodlands Indians ate?**

   A. They only ate vegetables.

   B. The ocean and the woods were full of fish and animals for them to eat.

   C. They traded with Europeans for food.

   D. They often starved because they could not find food.

5. **What are *boundaries*?**

   A. lines to separate one territory from another

   B. areas of the forest that were cleared with fire

   C. places where men from different groups hunted deer

   D. long houses that Woodlands Indians built

Name _____  Date _____

Comprehension Skill: Noting Details

# Life in the West

Paying close attention to the facts and descriptions in your textbook can help you gain a better understanding of what you are studying. This process is called **noting details.**

1.  **Read the sections called "Hunters and Gatherers" and "Tell Me More" on pages 59-60. Then write a very brief answer to this question: "How did the Native Americans of the Pacific Northwest celebrate special occasions?"**

    _____

2.  **Now, give a more complete answer to the question. You can do this by finding details about the Northwest Indians' celebrations. Review the section and answer the questions in the chart. You do not need to write complete sentences in the Answer column.**

| Question | Answer |
|---|---|
| What was this celebration called? | |
| What kinds of occasions did this celebration honor? | |
| What did people wear for the celebration? | |
| What did people do during the celebration? | |

3.  **Now use the details you wrote in the chart above to write a paragraph that answers the question: "How did the Native Americans of the Pacific Northwest celebrate special occasions?" Make your paragraph as detailed as you can.**

    _____

    _____

    _____

    _____

Reading and Vocabulary Strategies

Name _____ Date _____

# Life in the West

Review pages 58-63 to answer these questions. Choose the best answer. Circle the letter next to your choice.

1. **Why did the Makah Indians prosper?**
   A. because they could grow enough corn to trade with other groups
   B. because the ocean was full of whales they could hunt
   C. because their leader was fierce and conquered many peoples
   D. because they found minerals on their land

2. **Which did the Western Indians NOT need to do?**
   A. farm
   B. hunt
   C. fish
   D. gather

3. **What is a *drought*?**
   A. the name of a home built by Western Indians
   B. a long growing season that provides many crops
   C. the writing done by certain Native American people
   D. a long period of time with almost no rain

4. **What is a *potlatch*?**
   A. a special kind of soup made by the Plains Indians
   B. a celebration with gifts, singing, and feasting
   C. a large dinner where only corn is served
   D. a big hole dug to hide a child's gifts and treasures

5. **How did the Plains Indians live?**
   A. They followed the trails of animals and hunted buffalo.
   B. They built their homes deep in the forest, protected from other people.
   C. They often hunted and fished with other groups of Native Americans.
   D. They lived in old homes left behind by other Native American groups.

Name _____ Date _____

# The First Americans

Review pages 34-67 to answer these questions. Choose the best answer. Circle the letter next to your choice.

1. **How do most archaeologists believe the first people came to the Americas from Asia?**

   A. on foot or by boat

   B. by swimming

   C. by skating across ice

   D. by riding on animals

2. **How did the first settlers in North America hunt bison?**

   A. They dug big holes and chased the bison into them.

   B. They used large spears with spearheads made of flint.

   C. They clubbed bison over their heads with large rocks.

   D. They chased and stampeded the bison over cliffs.

3. **When large mammals slowly died out, how did people have to adapt?**

   A. They made bows and arrows to hunt smaller animals.

   B. They saved all their old bison horns and bones for tools.

   C. They moved to new places to find other large mammals.

   D. Early people starved and died out, like the large mammals.

4. **Which plant was found by Native Americans 5,000 years ago that has influenced people worldwide?**

   A. tomatoes

   B. lima beans

   C. corn

   D. bananas

5. **Which was developed by the Maya culture?**

   A. accurate calendars and a picture language

   B. the wheel

   C. work done by animals

   D. the first army to use armor

Name _____ Date _____

6. **What is an *empire*?**

   A. a business that makes products that can be sold to other people

   B. a town filled with immigrants

   C. a farming community

   D. land and people

7. **How did the Creek plan their towns and villages?**

   A. They built their homes around a central plaza.

   B. They built their homes in a long line through the forest.

   C. They built their homes on islands in the middle of lakes.

   D. They built their homes all through the forest with great distances in between.

8. **What is a *confederacy*?**

   A. a type of Native American home

   B. a special kind of clothing made by the Creek

   C. a large group made up of smaller groups

   D. a group of Native American leaders

9. **How did the Plains Indians travel?**

   A. by foot

   B. by buffalo

   C. by horse

   D. by wagon

10. **How did Southwest Indians get their food?**

    A. by hunting

    B. by farming

    C. by fishing

    D. by traveling around

Name _____     Date _____

Comprehension Skill: Summarizing Long Passages

# Trading Across Oceans and Continents

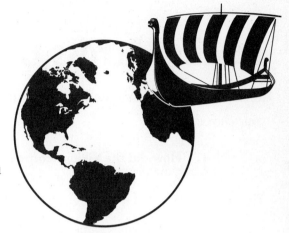

Writing a summary of what you have read can help you remember the important ideas. A **summary** is a brief statement of the main ideas in your own words.

**Start by looking again at the first Focus question in this lesson (on page 74, under the heading "Vikings Cross the Atlantic"). Write that Focus question here.**

1.  **Focus question:** _____

**As you read, jot down facts and details that help answer the Focus question. For example, you might want to note *how* and *where* the Vikings traveled, *what* they were seeking, and *who* their leader was.**

2.  **Notes:** _____

    _____

    _____

    _____

**Finally, summarize what you have read about the Viking explorations by writing one or two sentences that answer the Focus question.**

3.  **Summary:** _____

    _____

    _____

    _____

Name _____  Date _____

# Trading Across Oceans and Continents

Review pages 73-78 to answer these questions. Choose the best answer. Circle the letter next to your choice.

1.  **How did the Vikings come to North America?**

    A.  Wars between the Vikings and other Europeans brought them to Canada.

    B.  The king of Sweden sent the Vikings to North America to find gold.

    C.  Vikings came to North America to meet the Native Americans there.

    D.  Vikings traveled by boat from Iceland to Greenland to Newfoundland.

2.  **Who was Leif Ericson?**

    A.  a Viking trader who traveled to China to trade for silk

    B.  a skilled Viking woodcarver who worked on ships for the king

    C.  a famous musician who often entertained Vikings

    D.  the leader of a group of Vikings who landed on Canada's coast

3.  **How did trade lead to the rise of Timbuktu?**

    A.  Traders liked to travel to the Sahara.

    B.  Timbuktu was in the cool, beautiful mountains.

    C.  Trade brought wealth and people to the city.

    D.  People could trade silver for silk in Timbuktu.

4.  **Who was Mansa Musa?**

    A.  an Arabian trader who visited Cairo

    B.  a West African leader who ruled the kingdom of Mali

    C.  the name of a group of Native Americans

    D.  the leader of a group of Vikings who traveled to Asia

5.  **What is a *mosque*?**

    A.  an island found in the North Atlantic

    B.  something Arab traders wanted from the Chinese

    C.  a Muslim house of worship

    D.  a great center of trade and learning

Name _____ Date _____

## Gathering Information in the Media

# Stay Informed

Read this news article about the January Blizzard of 1996.

**Blizzard Strikes East Coast**

WASHINGTON — A powerful blizzard which began Saturday continues in its third day up the Eastern Seaboard. Record snowfalls have been recorded in several states, including 30 inches of snow in Philadelphia, Pennsylvania.

Airports have been closed from Washington to Boston, stranding thousands of travelers. In Washington, D.C., the federal government was shut down. In New York, the United Nations was closed. There have been at least 30 weather-related deaths. This is the worst winter storm to strike the East Coast in 50 years.

1. **Answer the questions to help you analyze and understand the news article.**

    **What is the subject?** _____

    **When did it happen?** _____

    **Where did it happen?** _____

    **What were some of the major events?** _____

    _____

2. **Why would a person on the East Coast want to know about this storm?**

    _____

3. **Why might the storm information be important to a person in another part of the country?**

    _____

    _____

Name _____  Date _____

Gathering Information in the Media

# Comparing Media Sources

Choose a news event that interests you. _____

Find information about your topic from two different media sources, such as a newspaper, a magazine, television, radio, or a computer on-line service. Record your information in the chart below.

| | Media Source 1 | Media Source 2 |
|---|---|---|
| What important facts did you learn about your topic? | | |
| Were any opinions given? What were they? | | |
| What were the advantages of using this source? | | |
| Were there any disadvantages? Explain. | | |

Name _____ Date _____

## Vocabulary Skill: Greek and Latin Roots

# Trade Brings New Ideas

Many English words have Greek or Latin **roots,** or origins.
Knowing these roots can help you figure out unfamiliar words. The
charts below show some Latin and Greek root words, what they
mean, and examples of words that come from them.

| Latin Root | Meaning | English word |
|---|---|---|
| *altus* | "high" | *altimeter* ("an instrument for measuring elevation") |
| *navis* | "ship" | *naval* ("of or about ships or a navy") |
| *specere* | "to look at" | *spectacle* ("a public display") |

| Greek Root | Meaning | English word |
|---|---|---|
| *astro* | "star" | *astronomy* ("the study of the universe beyond the earth") |
| *logy* | "speech, study or reason" | *biology* ("the study of life") |

**Circle the Greek or Latin root word in each word in dark type. Then match the
words with their definitions by drawing lines between them.**

1. **astronaut**      a.  the study of the earth

2. **spectacles**      b.  a nation's warships

3. **geology**       c.  a person trained to pilot a spacecraft

4. **navy**       d.  eyeglasses

**The words below appear in Lesson 2. Circle the Greek or Latin root in each.
Based on the meaning of the root plus the context in which the word appears,
write a definition for each word. Check your answers in a dictionary.**

5. **astrolabe** (page 84) _____

6. **navigation** (page 85) _____

7. **inspect** (page 82—"Silk Making in China") _____

8. **altitude** (page 84) _____

9. **logical** (page 85) _____

Name _____ Date _____

# Trade Brings New Ideas

Review pages 80-85 to answer these questions. Choose the best answer. Circle the letter next to your choice.

1. **How did the three Polos convince the rest of the family that they were their missing relatives?**
   A. They had birth certificates telling when they were born.
   B. They showed pictures of their parents from long ago.
   C. They cut open the linings of their coats, and jewels fell to the ground.
   D. They knew the secret code that only their family knew.

2. *Merchants* **are people who—**
   A. unwind silk cocoons by soaking them in water
   B. weave beautiful clothes from silk
   C. make their living by buying and selling goods
   D. produce literature, buildings, and fine works of art

3. **Who was Kublai Khan?**
   A. a wealthy trader in North Africa
   B. a 17-year-old who traveled to China
   C. the emperor of China
   D. a Greek thinker

4. **What are** *Arabic numerals***?**
   A. the same things as Roman numerals
   B. the way of writing numbers that is used in western countries
   C. a way of writing numbers from right to left
   D. a way of writing numbers used only in Arabia

5. **What was the** *Renaissance***?**
   A. the rebuilding of Cordoba
   B. a great rebirth of learning and creativity
   C. the name of a famous painting by Michelangelo
   D. a group that followed the writings of Aristotle

Name _____    Date _____

# The World of Africa, Asia, & Europe

Review pages 72-87 to answer these questions. Choose the best answer. Circle the letter next to your choice.

1. **What are *sagas*?**
    A. ancient stories of Iceland
    B. the prized tusks of walruses
    C. small ships from Scandinavia
    D. islands in the Atlantic Ocean

2. **The Vikings originally came from—**
    A. Africa
    B. South America
    C. Scandinavia
    D. Asia

3. **What did the Vikings find in Greenland that made them want to stay?**
    A. farmland
    B. ivory from walrus
    C. gold and silver
    D. horses

4. **Why was the unearthing of the Viking settlement in 1961 important?**
    A. This discovery proved that the Vikings and Native Americans were friends.
    B. Before then, no one knew for sure whether Vikings had been to North America.
    C. The archaeologists found out that Vikings made beautiful jewelry.
    D. Riches from the kings of Norway and Denmark were found in the settlement.

5. **What is *Islam*?**
    A. an islander who moves to another country for a better life
    B. a religion based on the belief in one God and the prophet Muhammad's teachings
    C. an organization to help traders increase sales and profits
    D. a group of religious leaders and businessmen working towards peace

6.  **What is a *pilgrimage*?**

    A.  a voyage across the ocean for the purpose of trading

    B.  a journey to a sacred place or shrine

    C.  a trip to a foreign land to learn more about that culture

    D.  the discovery of an ancient civilization

7.  **What did Marco Polo NOT see while he lived in China?**

    A.  gunpowder

    B.  Viking necklaces

    C.  coal

    D.  paper money

8.  **How did Marco Polo learn about China?**

    A.  Kublai Khan visited him in Venice.

    B.  He traveled to distant parts of China.

    C.  He was born in China.

    D.  He read about it in a book.

9.  **Who developed the city called Córdoba?**

    A.  the Chinese army

    B.  Marco Polo

    C.  the Muslims

    D.  Kublai Khan

10. **What was an *astrolabe*?**

    A.  a device used to measure the altitude of the sun and stars

    B.  a heavenly body found in space

    C.  an asteroid that fell to the ground in China

    D.  the very first attempt at a spacelab in ancient China

Name _____ Date _____

Comprehension Skill: Analyzing Assumptions

# Searching For Trade Routes

**Assumptions** are ideas that are accepted as true without proof. When people make assumptions, or "take things for granted," they accept something as true without thinking about it. It is important to identify assumptions so that you can decide if they are true.

Reread the first paragraph on page 89. It tells you an assumption about the seas that was made by sailors in the 1400s. Those sailors assumed that monsters lived in the seas. They made this assumption because they didn't know enough about the seas and because nearly everybody else believed in monsters too.

**Answer the questions below with complete sentences.**

1. **Reread the paragraph on page 92. What assumption did Christopher Columbus make about the geography of the world?**

   _He believed that he could get there by sailing west instead of east._

2. **What information was Columbus missing that might have led him to make a different assumption?**

   _Because he did not know there was a continent beetween asia_

3. **Have you or someone you know ever made an assumption that you later found out was not true? Write one or two sentences that explain what the assumption was, and what made you or the person you know question the assumption.**

   _____

   _____

   _____

   _____

Name _____ Date _____

# Searching for Trade Routes

Review pages 89-95 to answer these questions. Choose the best answer. Circle the letter next to your choice.

1. **Why did the Europeans come to America in the 1400s?**
   A. to reclaim their land
   B. to meet Native Americans
   C. to look for people lost at sea
   D. to trade and claim land

2. *Navigation* **is the science of—**
   A. studying the flow of ocean currents
   B. plotting and controlling the course of a ship
   C. making maps and using them to search for new land
   D. teaching sailors how to sail in foreign seas

3. **How did Portuguese sailors reach Asia?**
   A. by sailing north of Europe
   B. by sailing around the tip of Africa
   C. by sailing across the Pacific Ocean
   D. by sailing through the Mediterranean Sea

4. **Which Portuguese explorer reached India and found the first sea route to Asia?**
   A. Bartholomew Dias
   B. Prince Henry
   C. Vasco da Gama
   D. Christopher Columbus

5. **Who agreed to pay for Christopher Columbus's voyage to find a new route to the East?**
   A. the Tainos
   B. the Catholic Church
   C. Isabella and Ferdinand
   D. a group of Portuguese merchants

Lesson Review

Name _____  Date _____

Comprehension Skill: Understanding Sequence
of Events

# Spain Builds an Empire

The order in which events happen is called the **sequence of events**.
The events in history books are often told in sequence. Two types of
clues can help you figure out the correct sequence of events: **dates**, such as
September 6, 1492, and **time-order words**, such as *first, after, next,* and *then.*

1. **Reread the section called "Montezuma and Cortés" on pages 102–103.**
   **Write the time-order words or phrases you find on the lines below.**

_____

_____

2. **The events listed below are out of order. Review pages 100–105 to figure**
   **out the sequence in which the events occurred. Write a number on the**
   **line in front of each sentence to show the correct order.**

   _2._ Cortés took Montezuma prisoner and told him how to rule.

   _5._ Pánfilo de Narváez went to Florida to find the Seven Cities of Gold.

   _1._ Hernán Cortés reached the coast of Mexico.

   _4._ Cortés finished conquering most of central Mexico.

   _8._ Coronado and his men returned to Mexico after looking in vain for the
   Seven Cities for two years.

   _6._ Native Americans attacked Narváez and his army, leaving only four survivors.

   _7._ Francisco Vásquez de Coronado began an expedition to find the Seven Cities.

   _3._ Montezuma was killed and the Spanish took control of Tenochtitlán.

Name _____ Date _____

# Spain Builds an Empire

Review pages 100-105 to answer these questions. Choose the best answer. Circle the letter next to your choice.

1. **Which empire did Cortés defeat?**
   A. the Aztecs
   B. the Incas
   C. the Maya
   D. the Pueblo

2. **What is a *conquistador*?**
   A. an ancient weapon used by the Spanish
   B. a Spanish soldier
   C. a god worshipped by the Aztecs long ago
   D. a path explorers took from Florida to Puerto Rico

3. **How did the Aztecs record their history?**
   A. by telling their stories to their children
   B. by painting on cave walls
   C. by writing on paper in Spainsh
   D. by pictures painted on scrolls

4. **To *rebel* means to—**
   A. give in
   B. run from the enemy
   C. resist
   D. live peacefully

5. **What part of the Americas did Coronado explore?**
   A. Cuba
   B. the Southwest
   C. Peru
   D. Florida

Name _____ Date _____

Comprehension Skill: Understanding Cause and Effect

# The Columbian Exchange

A **cause** is an event or a condition that makes another event happen. The event that happens as a result is an **effect**. Here is an example of a **cause-and-effect** relationship from page 107: "To meet the growing demand for sugar, the Spanish built large farms called plantations."

| | |
|---|---|
| **Cause:** There was a growing demand for sugar. | **Effect:** The Spanish built large sugar plantations. |

1. **Reread the second paragraph on page 107. Use the information in it to complete the chart below.**

| | |
|---|---|
| **Cause:** Native Americans were not immune to diseases the Spanish brought to the Americas. | **Effect:** Spanish Diseases killed Native and Africans were inslaved |

2–3. **Now reread the rest of the section called "Sugar Cane and Slavery" (through page 108). Use the information in this section to complete the cause-and-effect charts below.**

| | |
|---|---|
| **Cause:** Many enslaved Native Americans who were forced to work on sugar plantations died or ran away. | **Effect:** Spanish captured Africans and used them to plant sugar cane. |
| **Cause:** They died because of poor conditions in the ship | **Effect:** Many enslaved Africans forced to sail to the Americas died at sea. |

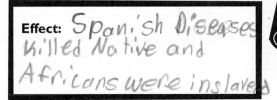

Name _____ Date _____

# The Columbian Exchange

Review pages 106-110 to answer these questions. Choose the best answer. Circle the letter next to your choice.

1. **What was the *Columbian Exchange*?**
   A. people that moved from Colombia to the United States
   B. people that lived in Colombia that wanted to change their lifestyles
   C. people, plants, and animals that traveled across the Atlantic after Columbus
   D. silk, spices, and gold that Columbus first brought to the Americas

2. **What is a *plantation*?**
   A. a place where plans for war are made
   B. a large farm where one crop is grown
   C. a boat that traveled to and from Europe
   D. a store where plants are sold

3. ***Immunity* means—**
   A. to run away from slave owners
   B. to work hard on a plantation
   C. to become a native of America
   D. to have resistance to a disease

4. **What happened to the African people when they were packed on ships and brought to America?**
   A. They were glad to be coming to the Americas.
   B. Many died from either shipwreck or disease.
   C. They took over the ships and returned to Africa.
   D. They gave in to the Spanish people and did not resist.

5. **Which of the following came from the Americas?**
   A. cows
   B. potatoes
   C. wheat
   D. sugar cane

Name _____ Date _____

Study Skill: Making an Outline

# Challenges to Spain

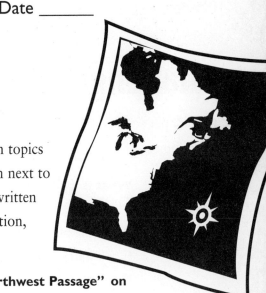

**Outlining** is a way of taking organized notes. In an outline, main topics are written next to Roman numerals (I, II). Subtopics are written next to capital letters (A, B). Important details related to subtopics are written next to Arabic numerals (1, 2). If there are no subtopics in a section, the important details are written next to capital letters.

**The outline below is from the section called "The Northwest Passage" on pages 113–115. Reread this section. Then complete the outline.**

**Searching for the Northwest Passage**

I. **England's Search**

    A. **John Cabot reached Newfoundland in 1497 and thought he was near China.**

    B. **Europeans believed there was a waterway that led to Asia.**

II. **France's Search**

    A. _____

       1. **In 1534, he sailed up a river known today as the St. Lawrence.**

       2. **He thought the St. Lawrence led to Asia.**

       3. **He tried two more times to find the Northwest Passage.**

    B. _____

       1. **From 1603–1608, he sailed up the St. Lawrence River.**

       2. _____

III. _____

    A. _____

       1. **In 1609 the Dutch sent him to find the Northwest Passage.**

       2. _____

       3. _____

    B. _____

Reading and Vocabulary Strategies

Workbook for Reading and Review   **39**

Name _____  Date _____

# Challenges to Spain

Review pages 111-115 to answer these questions. Choose the best answer. Circle the letter next to your choice.

1. **What is a *privateer*?**
   A. a captain of an armed, privately owned ship
   B. a private servant in Europe
   C. a knight in Queen Elizabeth's court
   D. a type of dish made privately by a silversmith

2. **Which was NOT a cause of the Battle of the Spanish Armada?**
   A. English attacks on Spanish ships
   B. the Spanish desire to conquer more lands
   C. the knighting of Francis Drake
   D. the search for gold in Africa

3. **What does the word *armada* mean in Spanish?**
   A. soldiers
   B. fish
   C. fleet
   D. ocean

4. **What was the *Northwest Passage*?**
   A. a bridge built between Greenland and Canada
   B. an underground tunnel that was a passageway to riches
   C. a discovery made by Christopher Columbus
   D. a water route through North America

5. **Who was Henry Hudson?**
   A. the governor of the first settlement in New England
   B. an English captain for whom a river and bay are named
   C. a European explorer who discovered Florida
   D. an enslaved African who became an explorer

Name _____ Date _____

Using Degrees and Minutes

# Voyage Through a Continent

This map is of Marquette and Joliet's return voyage in 1673. Its latitude and longitude lines are shown in degrees and minutes. Use the map to pinpoint several locations on or near their return route.

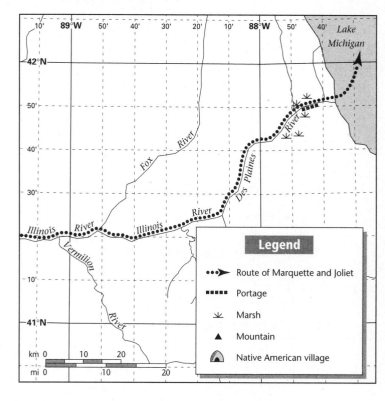

1. **Lightly color the map using blue for water, yellow for land, and red for Marquette and Joliet's route.**

2. **Write the name of the river or lake found at each of these locations:**

   a. 41°30'N, 88°10'W _____

   b. 42°00'N, 87°30'W _____

3. **Two symbols are missing from the map. Draw them in their correct locations:**
   a. Mountain (41°35'N, 88°10'W)
   b. Native American village (41°25'N, 88°50'W)

4. **On the map, find the portage — the place where the canoe must be carried. Write its location using degrees and minutes.**

   _____

Name _____ Date _____

Using Degrees and Minutes

# A Visit to Yellowstone

This map shows the first U.S. national park — Yellowstone. Most of the park is located in northwestern Wyoming.

1. **Lightly color the map using blue for water and green for park land.**

2. **Fill in the three missing minute labels on the map.**

3. **Write the name of the park entrance nearest each of these locations:**

   a. 45°N, 110°W

   _____

   b. 44°40'N, 111°10'W

   _____

   c. 44°10'N, 110°40'W

   _____

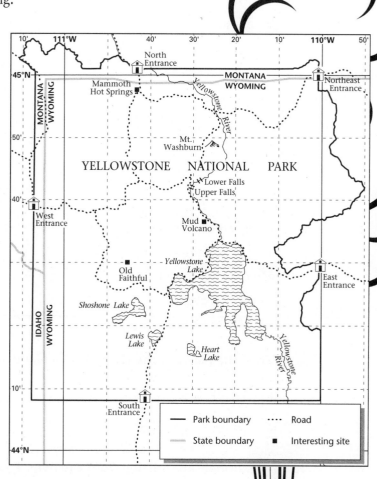

4. **Locate these sites using degrees and minutes.**

   a. Old Faithful _____

   b. Mammoth Hot Springs _____

Skills Workshop

Name _____ Date _____

# Explorers Come to the Americas

Review pages 88-119 to answer these questions. Choose the best answer. Circle the letter next to your choice.

1. **Which is NOT a navigating instrument?**
   A. compass
   B. cross staff
   C. astrolabe
   D. stopwatch

2. **What does *circumnavigate* mean?**
   A. to sail around the world
   B. to draw a circle on a map
   C. to travel from one town to another
   D. to make a boat go in circles

3. **Who did Cortés trick?**
   A. the Spanish soldiers
   B. Montezuma
   C. the Maya
   D. Esteban Dorantes

4. **What were the Seven Cities of Gold?**
   A. the seven capitals of the Maya and Aztec people
   B. seven large cities in Central America surrounding a gold mine
   C. legendary cities supposed to be the richest in the world
   D. the palace of the Aztecs with seven rooms filled with gold

5. ***Ambush* means—**
   A. to go to live in another country
   B. to enslave people
   C. to plant flowers and bushes
   D. to attack by surprise

Name _____ Date _____

6. **How did the African slave trade begin in the 1500s?**

   A. The African people started working for the Spanish in exchange for sugar.

   B. The Spanish wanted a mixture of people living on the plantations.

   C. The Spanish wanted to replace the Native American workers.

   D. Many of the Spanish returned to Europe and only the Africans were left.

7. **An *epidemic* is—**

   A. a need for food

   B. the transporting of slaves

   C. the spread of a disease

   D. the capture of slaves

8. **What effect did the transfer of plants and animals have on the people of Europe, Africa, and the Americas?**

   A. None of the plants or animals survived in their new environment.

   B. These new plants and animals were expensive, so only the wealthy got them.

   C. People in other countries did not like these strange foods and would not eat them.

   D. New foods and animals were introduced, and changed peoples' lives on all three continents.

9. **How did Drake defeat King Philip's "Invincible Armada"?**

   A. He fought King Philip's Armada on a day when there was no wind.

   B. He offered gold to the king's soldiers to destroy their own ships.

   C. He set fire to his own ships and sent them into the Armada.

   D. He attacked the ships at night when the crew was asleep.

10. **What were the results of England, France, and Holland's search for the Northwest Passage?**

    A. These countries spent much money and lost many crew members, but had a new transportation route when they found the Northwest Passage.

    B. The explorers didn't find a Northwest Passage, but new settlements were founded in the Americas.

    C. Many of the explorers died along the way, and the search for the Northwest Passage yielded nothing.

    D. When the explorers finally found the Northwest Passage, they found many treasures in this new land.

Chapter Review

Name _____ Date _____

Comprehension Strategy: Summarizing a Lesson

# The Growth of New Spain

When you **summarize** text, you restate in your own words the most important ideas you read about. Summarizing what you have read helps you understand and remember information. Use the following procedure to summarize Lesson 1:

**Step 1:** After you have read the lesson once, scan the text again. Then decide what the *topic* of Lesson 1 is. Circle the letter next to the best answer below.

> **Topic:**
> **A.** haciendas in New Spain    **B.** the colony of New Spain    **C.** the Pueblo

**Step 2:** *Reread* any parts of the lesson that confused you.

**Step 3:** Find the *main ideas* of the lesson. The main ideas on pages 122–123 have been written for you. Find two more main ideas on pages 124–125 and write them in the box below.

> **Main Ideas:**
>
> • New Spain had valuable resources, such as gold and lumber.
> • The Spanish claimed control over the land and the people of New Spain.
> • Native Americans were forced into the hardest work in the colony.
> • Spanish colonists owned haciendas where Native Americans worked.
> • Villages and businesses were built on the haciendas.
>
> _____
>
> _____
>
> _____

**Step 4:** Use the information you recorded in the boxes to write a *summary* of the lesson. Use another sheet of paper or the back of this sheet. Remember to include only the most important information in the lesson.

　　　　Workbook for Reading and Review　　**45**

Name _____    Date _____

# The Growth of New Spain

Review pages 121-125 to answer these questions. Choose the best answer. Circle the letter next to your choice.

1. **What is a *viceroy*?**
   A. a middle class group of people that lived in a colony
   B. a person sent by the king to rule in his place
   C. an older person in a community who gives advice
   D. a poor person with few skills

2. **Who were the *mestizos*?**
   A. Mexicans sent to rule in another land
   B. a group of nuns who lived in Mexico City
   C. children of Spanish and Native American parents
   D. rich and powerful people in Europe

3. **In the 1600s most people in New Spain worked on large farms called—**
   A. trade centers
   B. ranches
   C. haciendas
   D. colonies

4. ***Missions* are—**
   A. skilled workers
   B. valuable resources
   C. church settlements
   D. large ranches

5. **Who was Don Juan de Onate?**
   A. a Spanish nobleman who claimed the southwestern United States for Spain
   B. a friar who wanted to help Native Americans
   C. the ruler of an agricultural people with strong religious beliefs
   D. the viceroy of Mexico City

Name _____ Date _____

*Places and Regions*

# What Do Southwestern Place Names Tell Us?

Place names reveal information about the geography and people of a region. Places in the Southwest are rich in Native American and Spanish influences.

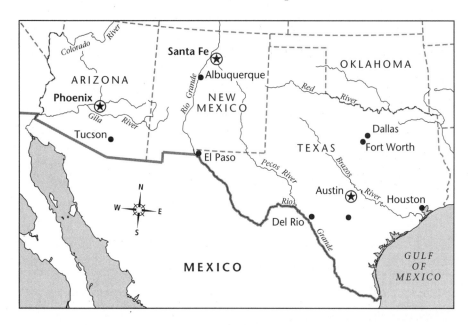

Use the map above to answer the following questions. Write your answers on the map and below.

1. **Locate and label San Antonio, Texas, on the map.**

2. **Find Del Rio, Texas, on the map. The name means "of the river" in Spanish. On which river is Del Rio located?** _____

3. **When the Spanish reached the Rio Grande in 1519, they called it Rio de las Palmas, which means "river of the palms" in Spanish. The Mexican name for the river is Rio Bravo, which means "great river" or "wild river." What do these names tell you about the river and the climate of its valley?**

_____

_____

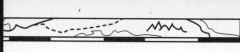

Name _____ Date _____

# Settling Across an Ocean

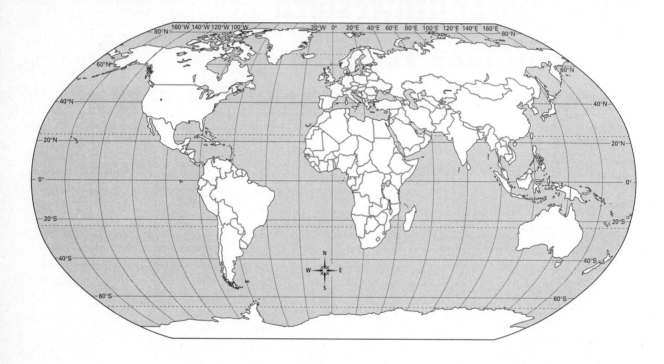

Answer the following questions on the map above.

1. **Using a different color for each country, shade in England, Spain, the Netherlands, and France. Make a key.**

2. **Locate and label the cities of New York, Quebec, Havana, and Boston.**

3. **Draw an arrow connecting each city to the country that first settled it.**

Name _____ Date _____

Study Skill: Examining Visuals as Part of Previewing

# The First English Settlements

**Visuals** are the maps, illustrations, photographs, and diagrams that are included in textbooks. You can learn more about the subject of a lesson by examining the visuals that go with it.

**Look at the illustration on page 128. John White made this drawing in the 1500s. Use the illustration to answer the question below.**

1. **What methods and tools did the Algonquin people use to catch fish?**

   A canoe and spears

**Look at the illustration of an Algonquin village on page 129. Complete the items below.**

2. **Describe the homes the Algonquin people lived in.**

   Small not coverend made with poles and red matting.

3. **Describe what the people in the illustration are doing.**

   working, building fire, and cooking

4. **Name something else you learned about the Algonquin villagers by examining this illustration.**

   They liked to dance and play music.

5. **Look at the illustration of Jamestown on page 130. List three things you learned about Jamestown by examining this illustration.**

   James town was small, near the sea, and had tiny houses.

Name _____ Date _____

# The First Settlements

Review pages 128-131 to answer these questions. Choose the best answer. Circle the letter next to your choice.

1. **What is a *charter*?**
   A. the rental of a boat or plane for a period of time in the new land
   B. a written document giving someone the right to establish a colony
   C. a part of a book written for a specific purpose
   D. the line that separates the territory of one colony from another

2. **Who were *indentured servants*?**
   A. people who worked in the offices of dentists in Jamestown
   B. many of the wealthy merchants that came to Jamestown to make money
   C. colonists looking for people who could work hard
   D. people who worked for several years in exchange for the trip to America and food and shelter

3. **Where did the first Africans in Jamestown work?**
   A. on rice farms
   B. on wheat farms
   C. on tobacco farms
   D. as slaves on plantations

4. **Who were most of the colonists who came to Jamestown, Virginia?**
   A. farmers
   B. soldiers
   C. missionaries
   D. gentlemen

5. **What was life like during the early years of the Jamestown settlement?**
   A. The colonists did not want to work hard.
   B. There was much free time and entertainment.
   C. From the start, most people people made a profit in Jamestown.
   D. At first, life was difficult and people starved.

Lesson Review

Name _____ Date _____

Comparing Primary and Secondary Sources

# Different Views

Who were indentured servants? What did they experience? Read these two different views to learn about them.

> *"A ship docked at a Virginia harbor in 1635, and from its decks emerged nearly two-hundred newcomers from England, among them twenty-five-year-old Thomas Carter. For some the voyage had cost over £5 sterling. For others, the price was higher still; several years of their lives. Carter, like thousands of other penniless Europeans, had sold himself into bondage as an indentured servant to pay his passage to the colonies."*

> *". . . since I came out of the ship, I never ate anything but peas, and loblollie (that is, water gruel). As for deer or venison, I never saw any since I came into this land; there is indeed some fowl, but we are not allowed to go and get it, but must work hard both early and late for a mess of water gruel, and a mouthful of bread and beef. A mouthful of bread . . . must serve four men, which is most pitiful . . . "*

a. _Secondary source_   b. _Primary source_

1. On the line below each selection, label it either **Primary Source** or **Secondary Source.** Circle the clue words in the primary source that let you know it was written by someone who experienced it.

2. How does reading both selections give you a broader view of the topic? _The first one tell you about the ship and the second one tell you about life on land_

3. If you were doing research for a report, do you think it would be wise to rely on just one primary source or one secondary source? Why?

   _primary resource because you know it's true._

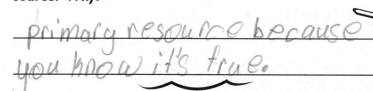

Name _____    Date _____

## Comparing Primary and Secondary Sources

# Hoop Dancing

These excerpts are from the book *One Nation, Many Tribes: How Kids Live in Milwaukee's Indian Community* by Kathleen Krull (Lodestar Books, 1995).

> *"Thirza Defoe, age eleven, can dance with 16 hoops encircling her slim figure. She is a solo hoop dancer, skilled in a centuries-old Indian tradition. . . . she performs on Indian reservations all around her home state of Wisconsin. She's danced in other states and as far away as Japan . . . . Thirza is half Ojibwa and half Oneida."*

> *"Sometimes when I dance, non-Indians come around and make fun of me with those whoo-whoo war cries they see in movies. It makes me mad . . . Kids should watch how we really dance, how we really act. Sometimes we sing along when we're dancing because we're enjoying ourselves—we might really like that song. We're not 'on the warpath' like in some old John Wayne cowboy movie."*

a. _____    b. _____

1. **Which selection is a primary source? Write your answer on the line below the selection. Circle the clue words in it that let you know it was written or spoken by someone who experienced it.**

2. **Underline key facts or opinions in each selection that you would use if you were to write a paragraph about Thirza Defoe.**

3. **How does reading both selections give you a broader view of the topic?**

_____

_____

_____

_____

Skills Workshop

Name _____    Date _____

Comprehension Strategy: K-W-L

# New England Settlements

In Lesson 3 you will read about the Pilgrims. The **K-W-L reading strategy** can help you think about and understand what you read. Here are the steps of this strategy:

K –   **Write what you Know.**  What do you already know about the Pilgrims? Write some information in the first column of the chart.

W –   **Write what you Want to learn.**  Write questions you have about the Pilgrims in the middle column of the chart. Then read the lesson to find answers to your questions.

L –   **Write what you Learned.**  After reading, write what you learned about the Pilgrims in the third column in the chart.

1.   **Use the chart below to follow the steps of the K-W-L strategy for Lesson 3. Then follow the steps below.**

| The Pilgrims | | |
|---|---|---|
| **K–What I Know** | **W–What I Want to Learn** | **L–What I Learned** |
| Religios People hard workers brave people | How many people came. How they cooked. How they built houses | How they dressed they died got help from Squanto |

2.   **Cross out any items in the "K" column that you have learned are not correct. Write the correct facts in the "L" column.**

3.   **Put a check beside each question in the "W" column that was answered by the lesson. Write those answers in the "L" column. Write an X beside each question that was not answered.**

Workbook for Reading and Review    **53**

Name _____ Date _____

# New England Settlements

Review pages 134-139 to answer these questions. Choose the best answer. Circle the letter next to your choice.

1. **Why did the Pilgrims settle in New England?**
   A. because it was too dangerous to sail around Cape Cod to get to Virginia
   B. because they liked the Native Americans they first met in New England
   C. because their ship landed on the coast of New England, and they were out of food
   D. because the land reminded them of the homes they left in England

2. *Puritans* **were given this name because they—**
   A. were in search of a pure and simple life
   B. liked to eat pure maple sugar
   C. were pure in the eyes of God
   D. wanted to purify the Church of England

3. **What was the** *Mayflower Compact***?**
   A. a book written to help new settlers in New England
   B. a box that contained important documents sent by the King of England
   C. a collection of plants, including a plant called the Mayflower
   D. a set of laws agreed upon by settlers who sailed on the Mayflower

4. **Massasoit was the leader of—**
   A. the Pilgrims
   B. the Mayflower
   C. the Puritans
   D. the Wampanoags

5. **Which was NOT a goal of the Puritans who settled in Massachusetts Bay?**
   A. to establish trade with King Charles I and make a profit
   B. to escape religious persecution
   C. to create a model community
   D. to establish a successful colony

Lesson Review

Name _____ Date _____

Comprehension Skill: Comparing and Contrasting

# French and Dutch Colonies

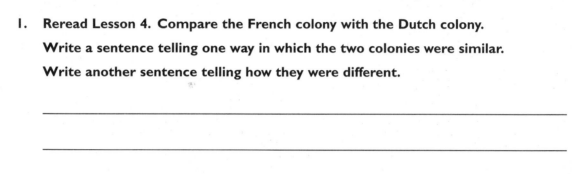

When you **compare** and **contrast** two things, you figure out how they are similar and different. Comparing and contrasting will help you understand what you read.

1. **Reread Lesson 4. Compare the French colony with the Dutch colony. Write a sentence telling one way in which the two colonies were similar. Write another sentence telling how they were different.**

_____

_____

_____

**Now look at the facts about the French and Dutch colonies below. Draw a line between each pair of related facts. Write S or D on the lines depending on whether the facts show a similarity or a difference. One line has been drawn and labeled for you.**

| **Colony of New France** | **Colony of New Netherland** |
|---|---|
| 2. Quebec was established near the St. Lawrence River. | a. New Netherland was founded the early 1600s. |
| 3. Colonists included Jesuits, fur traders, and farmers; most were French and Catholic. | b. New Amsterdam grew quickly. |
| | c. New Amsterdam was established near the Hudson River. |
| 4. New France was founded in the early 1600s. | d. Colonists included wealthy Dutch patroons; Norwegian, Swedish, Dutch, and English people; and people escaping religious persecution. |
| 5. Quebec grew slowly. | |

D

Name _____    Date _____

# French and Dutch Colonies

Review pages 142-147 to answer these questions. Choose the best answer. Circle the letter next to your choice.

1. **Who came to New France?**

    A.  plantation owners

    B.  priests, fur traders, and explorers

    C.  farmers and teachers

    D.  indentured servants

2. **What is a *pelt*?**

    A.  a container for carrying water on a ship

    B.  a sack for holding weapons and gunpowder

    C.  an animal skin with hair or fur attached

    D.  a kind of belt worn by Native Americans

3. **Where was New France located?**

    A.  along the entire coast of the Gulf of Mexico

    B.  just below Old France in western Europe

    C.  throughout farmlands in Central and South America

    D.  from the Great Lakes down the Mississippi River to New Orleans

4. **Why did different people settle in New Netherland?**

    A.  for religious freedom

    B.  to work as indentured servants

    C.  to gain wealth

    D.  all of the above

5. **Why were the Native Americans of New France eager to trade fur for metal tools?**

    A.  because metal tools could help them get more furs

    B.  because summer was coming and they didn't need warm furs

    C.  because fur was easy to get but metal tools were not

    D.  because the soldiers from New France forced them to trade

Lesson Review

Name _____     Date _____

# The Founding of European Colonies

Review pages 120-153 to answer these questions. Choose the best answer. Circle the letter next to your choice.

1. **Why did the Spanish establish missions in New Spain?**
   A. to convert the Native Americans to Christianity
   B. to produce wealth for Spain
   C. to conquer larger areas of land for Spain
   D. to protect the people from the Apache and Navajo

2. **What is a *presidio*?**
   A. a fort
   B. the president
   C. a Spanish settler
   D. a church

3. **Who led the Pueblo to burn churches and attack settlers and priests?**
   A. merchants
   B. Popé
   C. Juana Inés de la Cruz
   D. Don Juan de Oñate

4. **When Englishmen John White and Thomas Hariot were sent to a strange land, they—**
   A. became afraid and left one week after they arrived
   B. brought their sketchbooks and journals and recorded information
   C. took Native Americans back to England
   D. were chased back to the coast by the Native Americans who lived there

5. **What is the mystery of the Roanoke Island Colony?**
   A. The settlers disappeared without a trace, leaving behind all of their belongings.
   B. No one knows what happened to Virginia Dare, the first baby born in the colony.
   C. The king of England buried a treasure there, but it could be found by no one.
   D. Someone mysteriously killed the governor of the Roanoke Island Colony.

Name _____ Date _____

6.  **What does *invest* mean?**

    A.  to put money into a business
    B.  to ask someone to visit
    C.  to follow a large group of settlers
    D.  to write down on a piece of paper

7.  **In which year did the Pilgrims settle Plymouth?**

    A.  1776
    B.  1620
    C.  1685
    D.  1492

8.  **Who helped the Pilgrims by interpreting and teaching them to plant corn?**

    A.  Massasoit
    B.  Squanto
    C.  Pocahontas
    D.  William Bradford

9.  **What was a *patroon*?**

    A.  a wealthy owner who brought people and supplies to settle the land
    B.  an army that was very strong and powerful and never lost
    C.  a poor person that begged for a ride to North America
    D.  someone who hid on a ship out of desperation to get to New England

10. **What did the Dutch West India Company do to encourage settlement?**

    A.  gave away free food, clothing, and homes to people who would come to North America
    B.  guaranteed good-paying jobs to any settlers who would move to the new land
    C.  offered to send the children of settlers to the best colleges in the world
    D.  granted large land areas to wealthy people who would each send 50 settlers

Name _____ Date _____

Comprehension Skill: Topic, Main Idea, and Supporting Details

# Colonists on the Land

The **topic** of a passage is the subject it is about. The most important idea in a passage is called the **main idea.** A main idea is usually accompanied by **supporting details** that give more information about it. Reread the second complete paragraph on page 161. This paragraph contains a main idea and two supporting details:

| |
|---|
| **Topic:** the colonists' first impressions |
| **Main Idea:** When they first arrived, the settlers thought the land was a wilderness, but they soon learned they were wrong. |
| **Supporting Detail:** The Wampanoag, the Massachusetts, and the Pequot had cleared many areas for farming. |
| **Supporting Detail:** The Native Americans had burned forests and created meadows for hunting game. |

1–2. **Now reread the next paragraph. In the chart below, write two supporting details that help explain the main idea.**

| |
|---|
| **Topic:** Native Americans in New England |
| **Main Idea:** The Native Americans had abandoned much of this cleared land. |
| **Supporting Detail:** |
| **Supporting Detail:** |

3–5. **Reread the information about meetinghouses on pages 162 and 163. Write the main idea and two supporting details in the chart below.**

| |
|---|
| **Topic:** Puritan meetinghouses |
| **Main Idea:** |
| **Supporting Detail:** |
| **Supporting Detail:** |

Name _____   Date _____

# Colonists on the Land

Review pages 159-163 to answer these questions. Choose the best answer. Circle the letter next to your choice.

I.  **What kind of landscape did settlers find in New England?**

    A.  sandy deserts

    B.  dense forests

    C.  huge lakes

    D.  grassy plains

2.  **What was the first product the colonists sold for money?**

    A.  tea

    B.  maple syrup

    C.  wood

    D.  shoes

3.  **What effect did the glaciers have on New England?**

    A.  They made the soil richer and better for planting crops.

    B.  They brought mountains, which are today's ski resorts.

    C.  They created rolling hills and rocky shorelines.

    D.  all of the above

4.  **What was a *meetinghouse* used for?**

    A.  a marketplace every Saturday for selling goods

    B.  community activities, such as school and church

    C.  the fire station and police headquarters

    D.  the town's bank and post office

5.  **What does *self-sufficient* mean?**

    A.  feeling good about one's life

    B.  asking other people for help

    C.  being selfish

    D.  providing for all of one's own needs

Name _____ Date _____

## Comprehension Skill: Summarizing Short Passages

# New England Grows

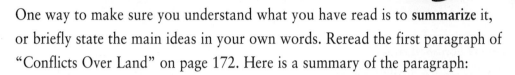

One way to make sure you understand what you have read is to **summarize** it, or briefly state the main ideas in your own words. Reread the first paragraph of "Conflicts Over Land" on page 172. Here is a summary of the paragraph:

> Native Americans helped the Pilgrims to survive when they first arrived in New England, and the two groups had good relations at first. This changed as other settlers came to New England.

**1–5.  Reread the rest of pages 172-173. Use the chart below to help you focus on the main ideas. Answer the questions in the chart. The first one has been answered for you.**

| Questions | Answers |
|---|---|
| **Who** had conflicts over land? | Puritans and Native Americans |
| **Where** did the two groups live? | |
| **What** were the conflicts about? | |
| **When** did the fighting first break out? | |
| **Why** did King Philip's War begin? | |
| **How** did the conflict end? | |

**6.  On another sheet of paper, write a brief paragraph that summarizes what you read. Use the information you recorded in your chart as a guide.**

Name _____ Date _____

# New England Grows

Review pages 168-173 to answer these questions. Choose the best answer. Circle the letter next to your choice.

1. **What does *banished* mean?**
   A. being forced to leave a place
   B. being told to practice one kind of religion
   C. not agreeing with others in a community
   D. living in a town with no government

2. **What is a *magistrate*?**
   A. someone related to the king of England
   B. a trader who sold goods to Native Americans
   C. the leader of a church in New England
   D. a person who led the government in a Puritan village

3. **Why were Roger Williams and Anne Hutchinson banished from Massachusetts Bay Colony?**
   A. They wanted to sing and perform, which was not allowed.
   B. They were found guilty of betraying the king of England.
   C. They wanted to marry people who were not Puritans.
   D. They expressed views that were different from the church.

4. **What is a *dissenter*?**
   A. someone who saves most of his or her money
   B. a person who disagrees with a leader's views
   C. one who settles a new land
   D. someone who tries to help other people

5. **Which colony was the first with true religious freedom?**
   A. Rhode Island
   B. Vermont Colony
   C. Massachusetts Bay Colony
   D. Plymouth

Name _____ Date _____

Comprehension Skill: Categorizing

# Making a Living

One way to keep track of important information when you read is to organize facts into **categories,** or groups.

Reread from the beginning of Lesson 3 up to the heading "Trading, Fishing, and Shipbuilding," about work in New England. Categorizing this information helps you understand and remember details about the work.

**1–3. Look at the chart below. Add at least one more job to each category.**

| Work done by women | Work done by men | Work done by children |
|---|---|---|
| • weaving cloth<br>• preserving fruits and vegetables for winter | • planting and harvesting crops | • bringing in fuel<br>• cutting potatoes for sheep<br>• feeding the swine |
|  |  |  |

**4–5. Reread the last two paragraphs under the subheading "Farms and Towns" on page 176. Fill out this chart using information from these paragraphs.**

| **Things colonists made at home:** | **Things colonists imported:** |
|---|---|
|  |  |

Name _____ Date _____

# Making a Living

Review pages 174-179 to answer these questions. Choose the best answer. Circle the letter next to your choice.

1. **Which does NOT describe a boy's life on a colonial Connecticut farm?**

   A. plants tea in the fields

   B. must rise early and do morning chores

   C. goes to school

   D. studies and cooks after school

2. **How were colonial homes different from many homes today?**

   A. They were much larger than today's homes, because families were larger.

   B. They had few windows, because glass was expensive.

   C. They were made of wood and kept out the cold better than today's homes.

   D. They let their farm animals live in their homes, rather than in separate barns.

3. **Where did children usually eat their meals?**

   A. sitting in small, child-size chairs

   B. outdoors on the porch

   C. sitting on their beds

   D. standing by a long table

4. **What is an *import*?**

   A. something important to the colonists for survival

   B. an item brought into one country from another

   C. a place where boats were kept

   D. the center of a colonial home

5. *Triangular trade* **took place between—**

   A. North America, South America, and Asia

   B. New England, the South, and the West

   C. North America, Africa, and Europe

   D. New England, England, and California

Lesson Review

Name _____ Date _____

Analyzing Change with Maps

# Mapping Time

Study these two maps of Boston Common and the area around it, then answer the questions.

1. **In 1722, the west end of the Common bordered on marshland. What does it border on today?**

   _____

   _____

2. **List any differences between the two maps. Choose one item and explain why you think it changed.**

   _____

   _____

   _____

   _____

   _____

   _____

   _____

   _____

   _____

   _____

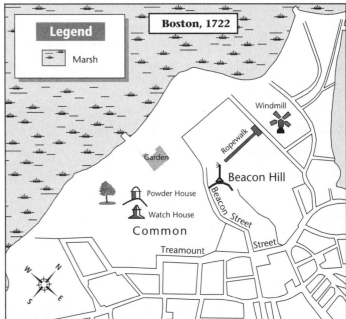

Name _____   Date _____

Analyzing Change in Historical Maps

# Take Me to the River!

Shown below are two maps of our nation's capital, Washington, D.C. The top map is a current map of Washington. The bottom map is a plan of the city drawn in 1800. Notice what is similar and what is different on these maps.

Look at the Potomac River on both maps. Notice how it has changed over the years. Part of the river was filled in to make more room for the city. Answer the following questions.

1. **How has the Potomac River area changed since 1800? Why?**

_____

_____

_____

_____

_____

2. **What two major avenues follow the same route on both maps? What appears to have happened to Delaware Avenue?**

_____

_____

_____

_____

_____

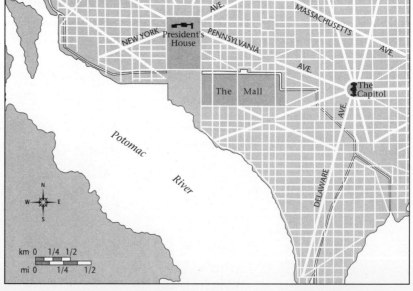

Name _____  Date _____

# New England Colonies

Review pages 158-183 to answer these questions. Choose the best answer. Circle the letter next to your choice.

1. **Which was NOT a natural resource found in colonial New England?**
   A. rich soil
   B. fish
   C. trees
   D. water

2. **What happened to many Native Americans before the colonists came to New England?**
   A. Much of the Native American population died of diseases brought by Europeans.
   B. Many Native Americans were glad to meet the colonists to trade with them.
   C. Most Native Americans had moved from New England to a warmer climate.
   D. Many Native Americans had killed each other in wars and few were left.

3. **How did Puritan communities arrange their towns?**
   A. Along the outside of town were the jail, general store, school, and churches.
   B. Several families lived in each home, and a post office was in the middle of town.
   C. Towns were centered around a meetinghouse, and each family had a plot of land.
   D. Homes were built in the woods for protection from other settlements.

4. **How did religious disagreements affect colonial New England?**
   A. People couldn't agree on where the church should be built, so it was built outside the village.
   B. People didn't agree with the way the Puritans governed the town, so they moved to Native American villages.
   C. Not all people agreed with the Puritan leaders, so they moved away and formed new colonies.
   D. People stopped going to church, because they were afraid of being accused of witchcraft.

Name _____     Date _____

5. **What was the Great Awakening?**
   A. the ringing of a large bell at 5 A.M. daily to wake the village
   B. a new interest in the arts in New England in the 1600s
   C. the realization that land had to be preserved for future generations
   D. a renewing of religious faith in the 1700s

6. **What problems arose between the Puritans and Native Americans?**
   A. They argued about the price of corn.
   B. Puritans took and used land where Native Americans were living and hunting.
   C. Puritans and Native Americans could not live together in the same villages.
   D. They disagreed on how much food would be grown and distributed.

7. **What was *wampum*?**
   A. a form of money made from polished shells put onto strings
   B. a kind of Indian food made from ground corn and milk
   C. a beautifully decorated club made by the Wampanoag to use in battle
   D. an agreement stating ownership of land in New England

8. **What is the name of the war between Metacomet and his followers and the Puritans?**
   A. Puritans War
   B. King Philip's War
   C. Metacomet's War
   D. Wapanoag War

9. **Which products did NOT come from North America?**
   A. silk ribbons and coffee
   B. candles and soap
   C. dried beef and maple syrup
   D. rice and tobacco

10. **What was the *Middle Passage*?**
   A. when a boy turned fourteen and was considered to be an adult
   B. a road that went from Boston across the United States to San Francisco
   C. the trip across the Atlantic Ocean from Africa to the Americas
   D. another name for the Mississippi River

Name _____ Date _____

Vocabulary Strategy: Structural Analysis

# People Living on the Land

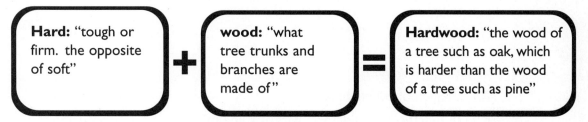

If you do not know a word's meaning, try breaking it into smaller parts.
A **compound** word is made up of two smaller words. You can often understand
a compound word if you know the meanings of the two smaller words.

**Look at the word *hardwood*, which appears on page 186:**

**Hard:** "tough or firm. the opposite of soft"

**+**

**wood:** "what tree trunks and branches are made of"

**=**

**Hardwood:** "the wood of a tree such as oak, which is harder than the wood of a tree such as pine"

1.  The compound words in the list below appear in Lesson 1. Draw a line to
    separate each compound word into two smaller words.

    **topsoil          livestock          freshwater          sawmills          gristmills**

Reread the sentences in which these word appear in Lesson 1. Then write
a definition for the following compound words. Check your definitions in
a dictionary.

2.  **topsoil** (page 186): _____

3.  **livestock** (page 186): _____

4.  **freshwater** (in a caption on page 187): _____

5.  On page 188, find context clues that help you understand the words
    *sawmills* and *gristmills*. Then draw lines to match the words *grist* and *mill*
    with their meanings.

    grist                      "grain that is going to be ground up"

                               "machinery that processes raw materials,
                                 or a building equipped with this machinery"

    mill                       "cotton that is used to make cloth"

Name _____ Date _____

# People Living on the Land

Review pages 185-188 to answer these questions. Choose the best answer. Circle the letter next to your choice.

1. **Which was NOT in the Middle Colonies?**
   A. Pennsylvania
   B. South Carolina
   C. Delaware
   D. New Jersey

2. **What is a *Piedmont*?**
   A. a region of rolling hills
   B. an unsettled or wilderness part of a colony
   C. a place where many pies are baked
   D. an area at the bottom of a mountain

3. **What is a *fall line*?**
   A. a place where all the rivers on the East Coast meet
   B. an area marked by steep cliffs that the colonists didn't want to fall from
   C. a line of waterfalls going up and down the East Coast
   D. the boundary between the New England Colonies and the Middle Colonies

4. **Which people settled in the Piedmont?**
   A. the English
   B. the Germans
   C. the French
   D. the Scots-Irish

5. **Why did farming become the main activity of the Middle Colonies?**
   A. The soil was fertile and good for farming.
   B. Many seeds were available in the Middle Colonies.
   C. There were many floods to water the crops.
   D. The people who moved to the Middle Colonies had been farmers in South America.

Name _____ Date _____

Comprehension Skill: Understanding an Author's Viewpoint

# A Mixture of Many Cultures

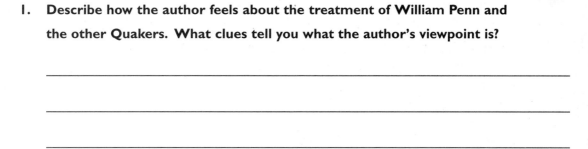

An **author's viewpoint** is how the author feels or thinks about the information she or he is writing about.

**Reread the paragraph on page 190, which begins "In the 1600s . . . ."**

1.  **Describe how the author feels about the treatment of William Penn and the other Quakers. What clues tell you what the author's viewpoint is?**

    _____

    _____

    _____

**Reread the third complete paragraph on page 191 and the "Tell Me More" feature at the bottom of the page. Then answer these questions:**

2.  **How do you think the author feels about William Penn's treaty with the Lenni Lenape? What clues help you figure out the author's point of view?**

    _____

    _____

    _____

3.  **How does the author feel about Penn's sons' treatment of the Lenni Lenape? How can you tell the author feels this way?**

    _____

    _____

    _____

Name _____   Date _____

# A Mixture of Many Cultures

Review pages 189-193 to answer these questions. Choose the best answer. Circle the letter next to your choice.

1.  **How did New York become a colony?**
    A.  The Duke of York took the land from the Dutch.
    B.  People from York, England, moved to America and began this colony.
    C.  Puritans moved south from New England and settled the land.
    D.  The Duke of York bought the land from the Spanish.

2.  **What is a *proprietor*?**
    A.  a person sent by the king to rule a colony
    B.  someone who frequently trades goods with another
    C.  an owner of land
    D.  a person who does not have a steady job

3.  **How did New Jersey become a colony?**
    A.  The Duke of York gave some land to two friends who started this colony.
    B.  The Duke of Jersey bought the land from the Dutch and founded this settlement.
    C.  People from Jersey, Germany, moved to this colony to have a better way of life.
    D.  The Dutch took this land from the Jersey Indians.

4.  **What is *religious toleration*?**
    A.  establishing a church at the center of a colony
    B.  allowing the church to run a colony
    C.  permitting weddings to take place in churches
    D.  allowing people the freedom to practice any religion

5.  **What does *Pennsylvania* mean?**
    A.  "Moving from Place to Place"
    B.  "Penn's Land of Peace"
    C.  "Brotherly Love"
    D.  "Penn's Woods"

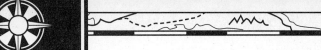

Name _____  Date _____

*Human Systems*

# What Did Colonial Americans Share?

American culture today is a result of the blending of immigrant, African, and Native American ideas for over 200 years.

Use the map at right to answer the following questions. Write your answers on the map and on the lines below.

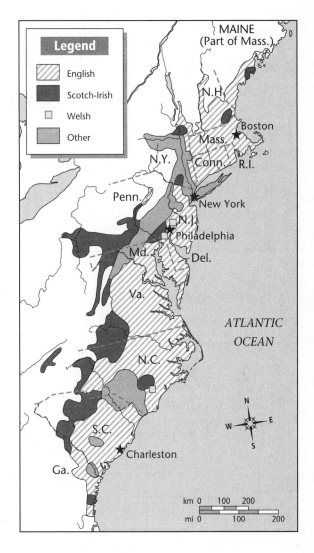

1.  **Which immigrant group was the majority in South Carolina?**

    _____

2.  **In which state or states were Welsh immigrants concentrated?**

    _____

3.  **Some immigrants chose to make their homes away from the coast, closer to the frontier. Identify at least one nationality that did so.**

    _____

4.  **Why do you think people chose to settle on the frontier? What would be an advantage and a disadvantage of settling away from more populated areas?**

    _____

    _____

    _____

    _____

Think Like a Geographer

Name _____    Date _____

# The Colonies and Their Products

1. **Find the New England, Middle, and Southern colonies. Label and color each group a different color.**

2. **Reread your text to find out what products were produced in each region. Use symbols to show these on the map. Create a key for your symbols.**

3. **How do you think the climate and natural resources of each region determined what it produced?**

_____

_____

_____

_____

_____

_____

_____

_____

**Legend**

——— Proclamation Line of 1763

– – – Colonial boundaries around 1776

Name _____ Date _____

Study Skill: Taking Notes

# Farm and City Life

**Taking notes** can help you understand and remember more of what you read. Here are some guidelines for note taking:

- Use the headings and subheadings in your textbook. They identify the topic of each section you read.
- Note the topic and main ideas of each section, and the most important details. The Main Idea sentences and Focus questions in your textbook can help.
- Don't try to write complete sentences. Just jot down key ideas and details so that you will understand them when you reread your notes.

**I-4.** **As you read Lesson 3, use the chart below to take notes on each section. Be sure to include information from illustrations, captions, and special features.**

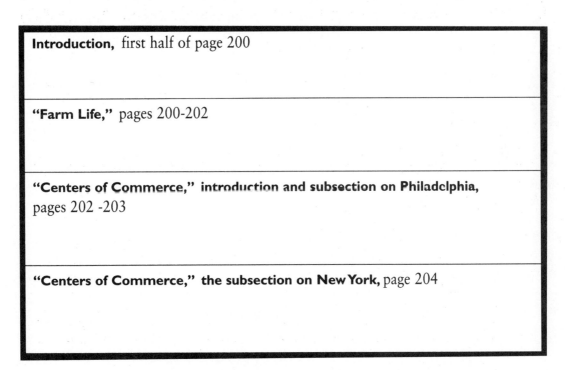

| |
|---|
| **Introduction,** first half of page 200 |
| **"Farm Life,"** pages 200-202 |
| **"Centers of Commerce,"** introduction and subsection on Philadelphia, pages 202 -203 |
| **"Centers of Commerce,"** the subsection on New York, page 204 |

Name _____  Date _____

# Farm and City Life

Review pages 200-204 to answer these questions. Choose the best answer. Circle the letter next to your choice.

1. **Where did most people live and work in the Middle Colonies?**
   A. in walled cities
   B. in mills
   C. on farms
   D. on ships

2. **Why were the Middle Colonies known as the Breadbasket Colonies?**
   A. Many of the workers in this region wove baskets for a living.
   B. Dairy products from this region were traded for other colonies' bread.
   C. Cows, chickens, and sheep were raised in this region.
   D. The farmers in this region grew large amounts of wheat.

3. **What was the *backcountry*?**
   A. an area next to a large city
   B. a low-lying area surrounded by higher land
   C. a settlement ruled by a distant country
   D. an unsettled, or wilderness, part of a colony

4. **What does *subsistence* mean?**
   A. taking care of the needs of one's community
   B. the minimum needed in food and shelter to support life
   C. an extra amount of anything, especially something people need
   D. the money people have to spend on themselves and others

5. **How was Philadelphia different from New York?**
   A. Log cabins were the only kind of house built in Philadelphia.
   B. Philadelphia was a planned city and had paved streets.
   C. Philadelphia was a much larger city than New York.
   D. Philadelphia was on a river, but New York City was not.

Name _____  Date _____

Reading for Cause and Effect

# Getting Results

Read this paragraph about one of Ben Franklin's civic projects.

> Ben Franklin was known for his many efforts to improve life in Philadelphia.
> One problem Franklin recognized was the problem of unpaved roads. In dry
> weather the roads were dusty; in wet weather they were muddy and hard to
> cross. To stir interest in the idea, Franklin wrote newspaper articles about the
> benefits of paved roads. Then he had a busy market street paved with stone.
> People liked the paved road. Next, he arranged to have the street cleaned.
> People liked having a clean street, and soon families and shopkeepers agreed
> to pay for the service. People who visited the paved road in turn wanted
> their streets paved. Soon the city was able to pave more roads because
> people were willing to pay a tax to support the cost of doing so.

1. **Find two cause–and–effect relationships in the paragraph.**
   **Write them here.**

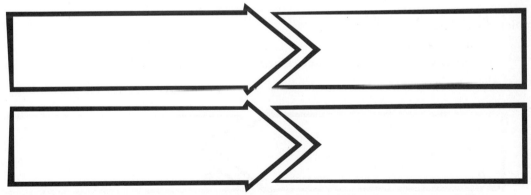

2. **Underline clue words in the paragraph that helped you find causes or effects.**

3. **What are two possible effects of Philadelphia's new roads?**

   _____

   _____

   _____

Name _____ Date _____

## Reading for Cause and Effect

# A Big Idea

When Ben Franklin saw a problem in Philadelphia, he worked to fix it.
His spirit of helping continues today in the Big Brothers/Big Sisters
program, which has helped over a million children.

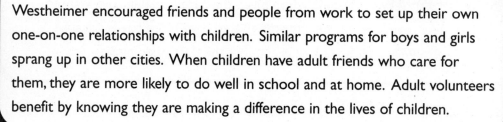

The Big Brothers idea began in 1903 in Cincinnati, Ohio,
when a businessman named Irvin Westheimer befriended
a fatherless boy. Westheimer saw the need for the child
to have an adult male for guidance and friendship. Because
he could see how his friendship had helped the child,
Westheimer encouraged friends and people from work to set up their own
one-on-one relationships with children. Similar programs for boys and girls
sprang up in other cities. When children have adult friends who care for
them, they are more likely to do well in school and at home. Adult volunteers
benefit by knowing they are making a difference in the lives of children.

Complete the following questions.

1. **Find two cause–and–effect relationships in the paragraph. Write them in
the flow chart:**

   a. 

   b. 

   a. 

   b. 

2. **Can a cause have more than one effect? Use examples from the paragraph
above to support your answer.**

   _____

   _____

   _____

**Skills Workshop**

Name _____   Date _____

# Middle Colonies

Review pages 184-209 to answer these questions. Choose the best answer. Circle the letter next to your choice.

1. **Which best describes the geography of the Middle Colonies?**
   A. dry plains
   B. high mountains and large lakes
   C. rolling hills and valleys and forests
   D. swampy land and savannas

2. **What effect did waterfalls have on the development of the Middle Colonies?**
   A. They were used for power for sawmills and gristmills.
   B. They were dangerous and kept trade from developing in the Middle Colonies.
   C. They attracted new colonists who were curious about the waterfalls.
   D. They cooled the temperature of the air and made the climate very pleasant there.

3. **How did the owners of New York and New Jersey want to make money?**
   A. by trading goods with Native Americans
   B. by renting land to the colonists for farming
   C. by building ships
   D. by selling British goods, such as tea, to the colonists

4. **Who offered religious toleration to the settlers and why?**
   A. the Quaker Church to gain more members
   B. the owners of New York and New Jersey to attract new settlers
   C. William Beekman to keep his land and jobs
   D. the Duke of York to strengthen his army

5. **How did Quaker beliefs affect life in Pennsylvania?**
   A. People went to jail even if they had not broken laws.
   B. Quakers shared what they had and lent each other money.
   C. Their beliefs made Pennsylvania a place of religious toleration and fairness.
   D. all of the above

Name _____     Date _____

6.  **Why did William Penn call his colony a *"holy experiment"*?**

    A.  It was governed according to Quaker beliefs and gave Native Americans a voice.

    B.  Penn believed that the Lenape people would convert to his religion.

    C.  All the people in Penn's colony had to attend church or be cast out of town.

    D.  If people believed as Penn did, his colony would be a model to England.

7.  **What is a *yeoman*?**

    A.  a self-sufficient farmer

    B.  an American colonist who opposed the British

    C.  a person who chooses to join the military

    D.  a wealthy merchant

8.  **How were backcountry farms different from farms in settled areas?**

    A.  In settled areas, only enough food was grown for the families who lived there.

    B.  Rice was grown only on farms in settled areas.

    C.  Cattle and sheep were raised on the backcountry farms.

    D.  In the backcountry, crops were planted among trees instead of in open fields.

9.  **Why did New York and Philadelphia become large and wealthy cities?**

    A.  Both were trade centers located on rivers and on harbors with access to the sea.

    B.  Both cities were owned by wealthy businessmen who opened furniture factories.

    C.  Both were governed by powerful landowners who helped these cities grow.

    D.  Both offered money and land to anyone who wanted to settle there.

10. **What is an *apprentice*?**

    A.  someone who learns a trade working under a skilled craftsperson

    B.  one who is recently freed from slavery

    C.  a person who moves from a farm to a city to earn a living

    D.  one who works in a line to make products that pass from one worker to the next

Name _____ Date _____

Comprehension Skill: Making Generalizations

# Geography of the South

Making a **generalization,** or a general statement, is saying something that is true for most people or in most cases. Generalizations are based on groups of related facts.

1. **The chart below shows three related facts about the tidewater region. Underline the generalization that is based on *all three* of these facts.**

**Fact:** The weather there is warm.

**Fact:** The region's growing season lasts up to eight months.

**Fact:** The region has plenty of rainfall.

Generalization

A. Many farmers grew rice in the tidewater region.

B. The tidewater region is ideal for growing crops.

C. Many colonists settled in the tidewater region.

2. **Read the facts in the chart below. Based on these facts, write a generalization about plantations in the South. Write your generalization in the chart.**

**Fact:** Plantations had many buildings and people.

**Fact:** Many plantations had workshops, storehouses, and blacksmiths.

**Fact:** Most plantations were near rivers to help ship crops to distant places.

**Generalization:**

Name _____ Date _____

# Geography of the South

Review pages 211-214 to answer these questions. Choose the best answer. Circle the letter next to your choice.

1. **What did the first colonists hope to find in Virginia?**
   A. gold and jewels
   B. good farmland
   C. many kinds of fish
   D. unusual plants and animals

2. **What is another name for *tidewater*?**
   A. water used for laundering clothes
   B. water with a salty taste
   C. the sea and its fish
   D. the coastal area

3. **How long was the growing season in the South?**
   A. all year long
   B. seven or eight months
   C. three or four months
   D. half a year

4. **What crop was very important to the farms in the colonial South?**
   A. corn
   B. wheat
   C. barley
   D. potatoes

5. **Who were especially skilled at growing rice in the South?**
   A. backcountry settlers
   B. tobacco farmers from Virginia
   C. farmers from Europe
   D. many Africans

Name _____ Date _____

Vocabulary Skill: Using a Dictionary

# Expansion of the Colonies

A **dictionary entry** for a word tells how the word is spelled, how it is pronounced, what it means, and what **part of speech** it is. Parts of speech are usually abbreviated in dictionary entries. Words in dictionaries are in alphabetical order and **guide words** at the top of each page can help you find words you are looking for. Here is one dictionary's entry for the word *bold:*

boisterous / bolt

**bold (bold)** *adj 1. Fearless and daring. 2. Too forward in manner.*

1. **Reread the first paragraph on page 215. Which meaning for *bold* is used in this paragraph?** _____

2–6. **Find out how each word in the chart below is used in Lesson 2. Then look up each word in a dictionary and complete the chart. Since some words have more than one meaning, be careful to fill in the chart with the meaning that makes sense in your text.**

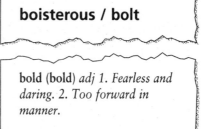

| Words | Guide words | Part of speech | Meaning |
|---|---|---|---|
| **invading** (page 215) **Hint:** Look up invade | | | |
| **charter** (page 216) | | | |
| **sound** (page 217) **Hint:** This word is capitalized in your textbook. | | | |
| **pitch** (page 218) | | | |
| **ban** (page 219) | | | |

Workbook for Reading and Review     **83**

Name _____  Date _____

# Expansion of the Colonies

Review pages 215-219 to answer these questions. Choose the best answer. Circle the letter next to your choice.

1. **What did the *House of Burgesses* do?**
   A. It was a place where extra crops were sold.
   B. It was the group of colonists who made laws for Virginia.
   C. It was the name of a large furniture company in Virginia.
   D. It was a farm where Virginia hogs were grown for ham.

2. **Why did William Berkeley set up boundary lines in Virginia?**
   A. to separate settlers from the Native Americans so they could get along
   B. to gain most of the profit from the tobacco grown there
   C. to keep English settlers from other colonies out of his land
   D. to show Virginians that order and organization would strengthen their society

3. **What did the first Navigation Act do?**
   A. provided equal rights for Native Americans
   B. helped colonists get easy passage across the sea
   C. limited colonial trade
   D. stated that all travelers must have passports

4. **Which was NOT an effect of Bacon's Rebellion?**
   A. Jamestown was burned to the ground.
   B. Relations between the Pamunkey Indians and settlers improved.
   C. Berkeley was forced to resign.
   D. Settlers were allowed to live wherever they chose.

5. **Who founded Maryland?**
   A. the Puritans
   B. the Quakers
   C. Lord Baltimore
   D. Henrietta Maria

Name _____     Date _____

Interpreting Flow Lines on Maps

# Go With the Flow

The flow lines on this map show colonial trade.

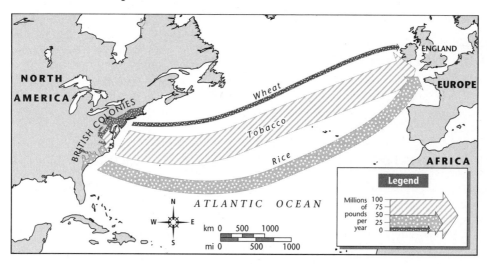

1.  **From where were these crops being shipped? Where were they going?**

    _____

2.  **By reading the legend, you can learn how many millions of pounds of crops were shipped per year.**

    a.  About 100 million pounds of which crop were shipped?  _____

    b.  About 10 million pounds of which crop were shipped?  _____

    c.  About how many pounds of rice were shipped?  _____

3.  **In addition to rice, the Southern Colonies shipped indigo, a blue dye. On the map, draw and label a flow line showing that one million pounds of indigo were shipped to England each year.**

Name _____ Date _____

Interpreting Flow Lines on Maps

# North American Immigration

This map is designed to show the 1994 immigration of people from five North American countries to the United States.

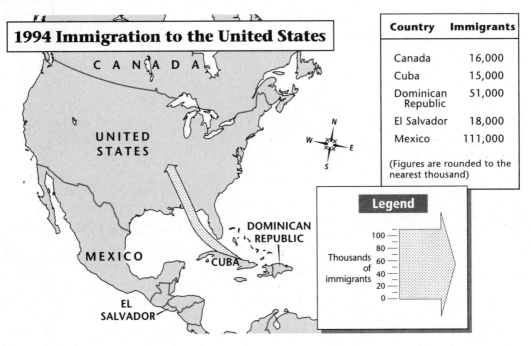

| Country | Immigrants |
|---------|-----------|
| Canada | 16,000 |
| Cuba | 15,000 |
| Dominican Republic | 51,000 |
| El Salvador | 18,000 |
| Mexico | 111,000 |

(Figures are rounded to the nearest thousand)

Answer the following questions on the map and on the lines below.

1. **Study the map, the table, and the legend to see how the thickness of Cuba's flow line corresponds to the number of immigrants. Use this information to draw the flow lines for the four other countries listed.**

2. **Which country had about half the number of people immigrating to the U.S. as Mexico did?**

   _____

3. **Which three countries had about the same number of people immigrating to the U.S. in 1994?**

   _____

Skills Workshop

Name _____ Date _____

Comprehension Skill: Comparing and Contrasting

# Agriculture and Society

You have learned that you can **compare** and **contrast** two things by thinking about the ways they are similar and the ways they are different.

**1–6.** Reread the section called "Plantations and Farms" and the "Tell Me More" feature on pages 224–225. In columns 2 and 3 of the chart below, take notes that answer the questions in column 1.

| | Plantation | Backcountry farm |
|---|---|---|
| What size was each type of farm? | | |
| Who did the hard labor? | | |
| What did men and women do on each type of farm? | | |
| What did farmers do with the harvested crops? | | |
| How did farmers get furniture and household goods? | | |
| What kinds of homes did the owners live in? | | |

Name _____ Date _____

# Agriculture and Society

Review pages 222-227 to answer these questions. Choose the best answer. Circle the letter next to your choice.

1. **What was a *post road*?**
   A. a route used by the postal service to deliver mail
   B. a road with light posts along it for travel at night
   C. a road with a post office at the end of it
   D. a series of telephone poles set up to help messages travel

2. **Which southern city was as large as northern cities?**
   A. Roanoke
   B. Williamsburg
   C. Charleston
   D. Atlanta

3. **How were plantations different from yeoman farms?**
   A. Plantations had less land than farms.
   B. Most workers on plantations were enslaved Africans.
   C. Women had no responsibility on plantations.
   D. Plantation owners paid higher taxes than yeoman farmers.

4. **Most Southerners —**
   A. lived and worked on plantations
   B. worked on farms in the backcountry
   C. owned enslaved people
   D. were enslaved workers who became free

5. **In which of these colonies were enslaved Africans the largest percent of the population in 1775?**
   A. Virginia
   B. North Carolina
   C. South Carolina
   D. Georgia

Lesson Review

Name _____ Date _____

# Southern Colonies

Review pages 210-229 to answer these questions. Choose the best answer. Circle the letter next to your choice.

**1. Why did farmers in the Southern Colonies concentrate on growing cash crops?**

A. Many of these farmers were poor and had to make money by growing as many crops as possible.

B. The climate, rich soil, and rainfall were ideal for growing these crops, which were in demand by other countries.

C. The farmers grew only as much as they could use, because storage was limited and food spoiled easily.

D. Whatever could be sold could be used to buy better equipment and provide improved methods of agriculture.

**2. What is a *cash crop*?**

A. a crop that reseeds itself

B. a crop grown to sell to other people

C. a crop that costs a lot to grow

D. all the leftover crops

**3. What was indigo used for?**

A. as a food to eat

B. as a medicine

C. to make a blue dye

D. to fertilize plants

**4. What is a *representative*?**

A. a person who speaks for others

B. someone who gives speeches for a living

C. one who sells goods

D. a person who delivers the mail

Name _____ Date _____

5. **Which was NOT a way that the growing of cash crops affected the societies of Virginia and Maryland?**

   A. encouraged the growth of huge plantations

   B. encouraged the use of indentured servants and enslaved persons

   C. allowed planters to enjoy a wealthy lifestyle

   D. provided trade opportunities for many Native Americans

6. **Why was Georgia founded?**

   A. as a debtor's colony and as a safe territory between Carolina and Spanish Florida

   B. to establish fur trading and to create a safe society for enslaved people

   C. for religious freedom and a place to produce supplies for the Navy

   D. so that King Charles I would have his own claim on land in America

7. ***Debtors* are people who—**

   A. don't agree with the government

   B. owe money

   C. want to be doctors

   D. trade furs

8. **What is a *trustee*?**

   A. someone who can be trusted to tell the truth

   B. a person sent by the king to rule a colony

   C. someone working for a more experienced person to learn a skill

   D. a person who manages something, like land or money, for others

9. **Which was NOT true about the post road that went from Maine to Georgia—**

   A. It made it easier for people to travel long distances.

   B. It still exists as part of a highway today.

   C. The south section was built first.

   D. Inns were built close to it.

10. **Which was NOT true about life on plantations?**

    A. Teachers lived on plantations and taught school there.

    B. Plantations were like small towns with their own blacksmiths and bakeries.

    C. Plantation owners bought only a few items that were imported from England.

    D. Most workers on plantations were paid and could quit if they wanted a new job.

Name _____  Date _____

Comprehension Skill: Topic, Main Idea, and Supporting Details

# The French and Indian War

Each lesson in your textbook has a topic, one or more main ideas, and details that support each main idea. The **topic** of each lesson is usually stated in the lesson title. The Main Idea sentence states the lesson's **main idea**. The main idea is supported by **details** in the lesson sections. Each section has a main idea and supporting details of its own.

1. **Write the main idea of Lesson I in the chart below. You can find it on page 235.**

> **Topic:** The French and Indian War
>
> **Main Idea:**

2–4. **Reread the section called "War and British Victory" on pages 238–239. Read the information already in the chart. Find the most important idea in this section and write it in the main idea box. Write two more details that support the main idea.**

> **Topic:** War and British Victory
>
> **Main Idea:**
>
> **Supporting Detail:** Britain declared war on France in 1756.
>
> **Supporting Detail:**
>
> **Supporting Detail:**

Name _____ Date _____

# The French and Indian War

Review pages 235-239 to answer these questions. Choose the best answer. Circle the letter next to your choice.

1. **Which is NOT a reason why tensions increased among the French, Native Americans, and British?**

   A. The French wanted the land for farming to support their growing colonies.

   B. The French wanted to defend their claims in North America.

   C. The British wanted a larger part of the fur trade and more land.

   D. The British wanted to farm land in the Ohio River Valley.

2. **What was Fort Necessity?**

   A. a French fort built to protect their people from the Native Americans

   B. a British fort along the American-Canadian border

   C. a fort to protect George Washington's troops from the French

   D. a fort where Americans stored and protected all their military supplies

3. **What is a _congress_?**

   A. a meeting of representatives

   B. a group of fur traders

   C. a group of Iroquois chiefs

   D. a place where people meet

4. **What are _allies_?**

   A. roads behind the homes of British settlers

   B. agreements to trade fairly with others

   C. land claims

   D. people who join with others for a specific purpose

5. **What is a _proclamation_?**

   A. a strong fort

   B. a battle cry

   C. an official announcement

   D. a meeting with Native Americans

Name _____  Date _____

Interpreting a Battle Map

# A Cliffhanger Battle

In 1759 British troops secretly climbed the cliffs leading to an area that lay outside the city of Quebec. There the British defeated the French and helped win Canada for the British Empire. Study the map to find out how the British were able to defeat the French.

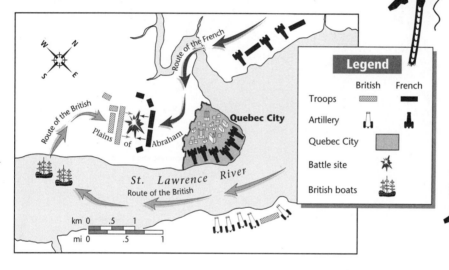

Answer the following questions.

1.  **Locate the Battle of Quebec on the map, and describe its location.**

    _____

2.  **Look at where the French artillery are located. Why do you think the British moved up the St. Lawrence at night?**

    _____

    _____

3.  **Once the French realized the British were attacking from the Plains of Abraham, they quickly moved to meet them. Look at the compass rose. In what general direction did the French troops move?**

    _____

Name _____  Date _____

Interpreting a Battle Map

# The Spanish Armada

On July 19, 1588, the Spanish Armada sailed from La Coruña, Spain, to lead an invasion of England. The English navy defeated the Armada in a series of sea battles. Study the map to find out how the English defeated the Armada.

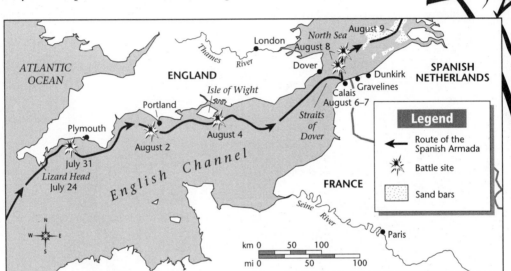

Answer the following questions.

1. **How many sea battles did the Armada fight before reaching Calais?** _____

2. **The most decisive battle between England and the Armada was near Gravelines. Where did the Armada go next?** _____

3. **Compare this map with the Battle of Quebec map on pages 240–241 of your textbook. How are they similar? How are they different?**

_____

_____

_____

_____

Name _____  Date _____

Comprehension Skill: Making Judgments

# Growing Conflict with Britain

When you make a **judgment,** you form an opinion about something. Your judgment should be based on facts and logic as well as your own thoughts and beliefs. You can use information from your textbook and your own experiences to make judgments about historical events.

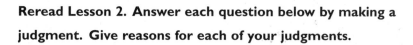

**Reread Lesson 2. Answer each question below by making a judgment. Give reasons for each of your judgments.**

The British government spent a lot of money to defend colonists during the French and Indian War. The government decided the colonists should help pay for this war.
Question: Was the British government's decision fair or unfair?

1. **My judgment:** _____

2. **Reasons:** _____

British citizens in England were taxed by their elected representatives in Parliament. The colonists did not have elected representatives in Parliament but still had to pay British taxes.
Question: Was the British government right or wrong to tax the colonists?

1. **My judgment:** _____

2. **Reasons:** _____

To protest the Stamp Act, many colonists burned stamps and covered stamp agents with tar and feathers. Soon no one would sell stamps anymore.
Question: Were the protests of the colonists right or wrong?

1. **My judgment:** _____

2. **Reasons:** _____

Reading and Vocabulary Strategies

Name _____     Date _____

# Growing Conflict with Britain

Review pages 242-245 to answer these questions. Choose the best answer. Circle the letter next to your choice.

1. **Why did Britain tax the colonies?**
   A. to bring more colonists to America from England
   B. to make more stamps to help deliver the mail
   C. to cover the costs of sending British troops to North America
   D. to stop settlers from moving to New England

2. **What is *Parliament*?**
   A. the selling of stamps
   B. the House of Burgesses
   C. Britain's law-making body
   D. a group of men from Boston

3. **What does *repeal* mean?**
   A. to sell
   B. to try again
   C. to buy again
   D. to cancel

4. **Which was NOT a response to the Stamp Act?**
   A. The Sons of Libery were organized.
   B. People stopped sending letters through the mail.
   C. Colonists burned the stamps and threatened the stamp sellers.
   D. Some stamp sellers were covered with tar and feathers by angry colonists.

5. **What is one way that the colonists resisted the Townshend Acts?**
   A. making their own tea from herbs and weaving their own cloth
   B. writing letters to the British government
   C. not attending meetings held in the town square
   D. raising money for the new government

Name _____  Date _____

# Background to the Revolution

Review pages 234-247 to answer these questions. Choose the best answer. Circle the letter next to your choice.

1.  **What did the French do to protect their fur trade?**
    A.  forced out the Iroquois
    B.  established legal boundaries
    C.  sent for more troops from France
    D.  built a line of forts

2.  **What was a result of the battle at Fort Necessity?**
    A.  Washington defeated the French.
    B.  Washington gained valuable experience as a military leader.
    C.  The British won the battle.
    D.  Many men became ill and died of disease.

3.  **What was the *Albany Plan of Union*?**
    A.  a plan to meet in New York to begin a new fur-trading union
    B.  a plan for helping the northern colonies to establish new laws
    C.  a proposal for uniting the French, British, and Native Americans
    D.  a proposal for joining the colonies together to fight the French

4.  **Which was NOT an effect of Britain's victory in the French and Indian War?**
    A.  Britain gained control of much more land in North America.
    B.  French ownership of land in North America expanded.
    C.  France lost land claims in North America.
    D.  Native Americans began to lose land to British settlers.

5.  **Which is NOT true about the Proclamation of 1763?**
    A.  It was a response to Pontiac's Rebellion.
    B.  Colonists wanted British troops to enforce it.
    C.  Colonists ignored it because they wanted new land.
    D.  It said that Native Americans owned land west of the Appalachian Mountains.

Name _____   Date _____

6. **What is a *tax*?**

   A. the cost of sending troops to the colonies

   B. money raised by the colonies

   C. money paid to purchase military supplies

   D. money people pay to their government

7. **What was the colonies' response to Britain's taxation?**

   A. Many of the colonists decided to move back to England.

   B. The colonists protested these taxes.

   C. The colonists were not happy, but they paid the taxes quietly.

   D. They bought many of the stamps.

8. **What was the *Stamp Act*?**

   A. All mail had to have a stamp printed by the British postal service before it could be delivered.

   B. Stamps had to be purchased to put on all paper goods, and this money went to the British.

   C. Everyone coming from another country to America had to pay to have a stamp on their hand to show where they came from.

   D. The king stamped his feet when he heard about the behavior of the colonists, and his new laws were named for this action.

9. **What is a *duty*?**

   A. someone who sold stamps

   B. a tax on imported goods

   C. a young lawyer

   D. things from England, such as tea and cloth

10. **What does *boycott* mean?**

    A. destruction of British property

    B. the training of boys who wished to become soldiers

    C. refusal to buy a product as a means of protest

    D. a way to raise money that the colonists agreed with

Name _____ Date _____

## Comprehension Skill: Analyzing Propaganda

# Crisis in Boston

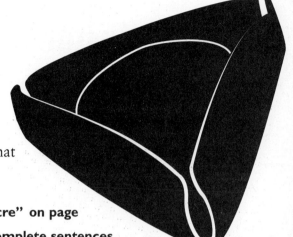

**Propaganda** is information used by a group to win support for a cause or to persuade people to do something. Propaganda often uses words and pictures that make people feel strong emotions.

**Reread the section called "The Boston Massacre" on page 250. Then answer the questions below with complete sentences.**

1. **Was the Boston Massacre really a massacre? Explain your answer.**

   _____

   _____

2. **Why did colonial leaders call the incident a "massacre"?**

   _____

   _____

3. **Why did colonial leaders want other colonists to think British soldiers were dangerous?**

   _____

   _____

4. **Look at Paul Revere's etching of the Boston Massacre shown on page 250. Read the captions. How do you think the etching might have been different if it had been made by an artist who supported the British cause?**

   _____

   _____

   _____

Workbook for Reading and Review **99**

Name _____ Date _____

# Crisis in Boston

Review pages 249-255 to answer these questions. Choose the best answer. Circle the letter next to your choice.

1. **What is a *massacre*?**
   A. the paying of a tax on tea
   B. a large area of land taken over by another country
   C. Parliament giving one company total control of an item of trade
   D. the killing of defenseless people

2. **What is *propaganda*?**
   A. information used to support a cause
   B. a way to punish those who break laws
   C. rebellion against another government
   D. unloading goods from a boat

3. **How did the Tea Act increase tensions between Britain and the colonies?**
   A. The Tea Act was a clever way to get colonists to buy taxed tea.
   B. It led to the Boston Tea Party, which in turn led to the Intolerable Acts.
   C. After the Tea Act, colonists began drinking American coffee, not British tea.
   D. It caused colonists to form an army and secretly attack the British in Boston.

4. ***Patriots* were—**
   A. colonists who returned to England as their patriotic duty
   B. colonists who joined the British army
   C. people who opposed the British government
   D. people who drank British tea

5. **What was a *committee of correspondence*?**
   A. a group that started the first newspaper in New England
   B. people who wrote to the governor in England
   C. people who wrote the laws
   D. people who shared information about the conflict with Britain

Lesson Review

Name _____ Date _____

Comprehension Skill: Recognizing Fact and Opinion

# The Fighting Begins

Remember that a **fact** is a statement that can be proven to be true or false. An **opinion** is a statement that tells what a person thinks or feels and cannot be proven. Here are a fact and an opinion from Lesson 2:

| **Fact:** | **Opinion:** |
|---|---|
| In 1775, a new British governor, General Gage, arrived in Boston with 5,000 soldiers. | The Intolerable Acts (called the Coercive Acts in England) were too harsh. |

**Reread the section "Moving Closer to Independence" on pages 264–265, up to the subheading "The Battle of Bunker Hill." Then complete items 1 and 2 below.**

1. **Write one fact about the Second Continental Congress that is given in this section.**

   _____

2. **In the opinion of delegates to the Second Continental Congress, what was George Washington like?**

   _____

**Reread each paragraph listed below. Then write *fact* or *opinion* after each statement.**

3. (page 266, first complete paragraph) **There was more fighting on Breed's Hill than there was on Bunker Hill.** _____

4. (page 266, third complete paragraph) **In his behavior toward the colonists, the British king acted like a tyrant.** _____

5. (page 266, fourth complete paragraph) **African Americans fought in the battles of Lexington, Concord, and Bunker Hill.** _____

Name _____ Date _____

# The Fighting Begins

Review pages 262-267 to answer these questions. Choose the best answer. Circle the letter next to your choice.

1. **What does *militia* mean?**
   A. an army of ordinary citizens
   B. the head officers of an army
   C. the beginning of a battle
   D. a war fought for independence

2. **What role did Paul Revere play in the Battle of Lexington?**
   A. He marched through town beating his drum to announce the battle.
   B. He led the Patriot army that defeated the British troops in that battle.
   C. He warned surrounding towns that the British were coming.
   D. He was a doctor who helped care for the wounded after the battle.

3. **A *delegate* is someone—**
   A. who joins an army
   B. sent to deliver a message
   C. chosen to represent a group of people
   D. who supports a cause

4. **What are *casualties*?**
   A. people one gets along with
   B. people killed, wounded, or missing
   C. people who sign up for the army
   D. people who win victories

5. **What was the colonists' response to the battles of Lexington, Concord, and Bunker Hill?**
   A. to continue fighting to separate from British rule
   B. to repeal the Intolerable Acts
   C. to become independent from other colonies
   D. to free African Americans

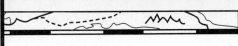

Name _____ Date _____

*Environment and Society*

# How Did Land and Water Affect a Battle?

At the Battle of Bunker Hill in Charlestown, geography was as important as soldiers and guns.

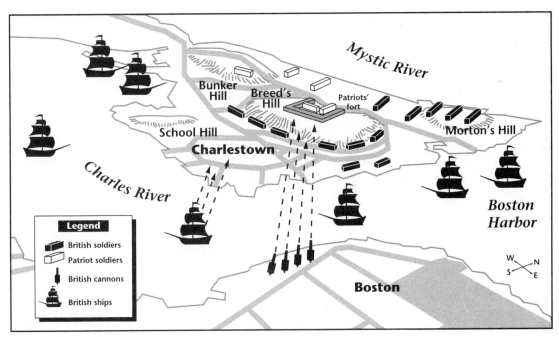

Use the map above to answer the following questions. Write your answers on the map and below.

1. **List the geographic locations important to the Patriots at the Battle of Bunker Hill.**

   _____

2. **Suppose the British had lost the battle. Find at least one route of escape they could have taken. Use dashed lines to mark the route on the map.**

3. **On the map, show the Patriots' route of escape. Why do you think more Patriots were killed or wounded during their escape than during the battle?**

   _____

   _____

Name _____ Date _____

# Revolutionary War Battles

One of the reasons the Patriots eventually defeated the British was because they used the features of the land on which they were fighting.

1. **Using your textbook, find and label six Revolutionary War battle sites.**

2. **Study the landforms around the sites. How might these geographic features have affected battles? The flow of soldiers and supplies?**

_____

_____

_____

_____

_____

_____

_____

**Legend**

———— Proclamation Line of 1763

– – – – Colonial boundaries around 1776

40°N

N
W · E
S

35°N

30°N

75°W

25°N

km 0    200    400
mi 0       200       400

90°W          85°W          80°W

Name _____  Date _____

Comprehension Strategy: Adjust Reading Rate

# Declaring Independence

When you read an enjoyable story, you can read quickly. However, you should read dense or difficult texts more slowly. Your textbook includes *quotations* (things that people said or wrote) and *excerpts* (parts) from historical documents. You should slow your **reading rate,** or speed, when you read these passages.

**Reread the section called "The Declaration of Independence" on pages 271–273.**

1.  **Think about the excerpt from the Declaration of Independence that begins "We therefore declare. . . ." This excerpt appears on page 272. In your own words, briefly tell what this excerpt means. If necessary, reread the excerpt more slowly to help you understand it. Write your description below.**

    _____

    _____

    _____

2.  **Next, think about the quotation from Abigail Adams in the middle of page 273. Briefly explain in your own words what Abigail Adams meant. Write your description below.**

    _____

    _____

    _____

3.  **Think about how quickly or slowly you read the excerpts from the Declaration of Independence and the quotations. Was your reading rate slower or faster than when you read the regular text? Explain why.**

    _____

Reading and Vocabulary Strategies

Name _____  Date _____

# Declaring Independence

Review pages 270-273 to answer these questions. Choose the best answer. Circle the letter next to your choice.

1. **What is a *petition*?**
   A. a person who owes money
   B. a written request signed by many people
   C. a person who speaks for other people
   D. extra money after expenses have been paid

2. **What was *Common Sense*?**
   A. a book written about democracy by Thomas Jefferson
   B. a book filled with advice for living written by Benjamin Franklin
   C. a newspaper written by the Sons of Liberty telling about Britain's actions
   D. a pamphlet written about independence by Thomas Paine

3. **Which is NOT part of the Declaration of Independence?**
   A. "Four score and seven years ago..."
   B. "We hold these truths to be self-evident..."
   C. "...among these are life, liberty, and the pursuit of happiness..."
   D. "...that all men are created equal..."

4. **When was the Declaration of Independence officially approved?**
   A. July 5, 1775
   B. June 7, 1776
   C. July 4, 1776
   D. June 7, 1775

5. **What is *treason*?**
   A. an army made up of ordinary citizens
   B. a reason to rebel against something one doesn't believe in
   C. to declare independence
   D. revolt against the government, betrayal of one's country

Name _____    Date _____

Interpreting Historical Documents

# Investigating the Past

Read this quotation from the preamble of the Declaration of Independence. It tells why the Continental Congress wrote the document.

> *"When in the Course of human events, it becomes necessary for one people to dissolve the political bands which have connected them with another, and to assume among the powers of the earth, the separate and equal station to which the Laws of Nature and of Nature's God entitle them, a decent respect to the opinions of mankind requires that they should declare the causes which impel them to the separation."*

1. **Break this quotation into smaller parts. Draw a slash mark (/) after each part. Example: When in the Course of human events,/**

2. **Write the definitions of the words or phrases below.**

   dissolve _____

   political bands _____

   station _____

   entitle _____

   impel _____

3. **Write the passage in your own words, focusing on each of the smaller parts.**

   _____

   _____

   _____

   _____

Name _____  Date _____

Interpreting Historical Documents

# In Ye Name

Copy a passage from one of the historical documents at the back of your textbook, such as the Constitution. Then follow these steps to interpret it.

1. **Historical document** _____

2. **Passage** _____

   _____

   _____

   _____

   _____

   _____

3. **Skim the passage to get an overview of what it says. Break it up into smaller parts. Draw a slash mark (/) after each part.**

4. **Rewrite the passage in your own words, focusing on each of the smaller parts. Look up any words you don't understand in a dictionary.**

   _____

   _____

   _____

   _____

   _____

   _____

Name _____ Date _____

# The Road to Independence

Review pages 248-277 to answer these questions. Choose the best answer. Circle the letter next to your choice.

**1. Which was NOT a cause of the Boston Massacre?**

A. tension between colonists and British soldiers

B. tea in the colonies

C. colonists throwing snowballs at soldiers

D. soldiers firing into the crowd

**2. What was a result of the Boston Massacre?**

A. Parliament repealed the Tea Act.

B. Britain took control of Boston, and angry colonists moved south.

C. The colonists used it as propaganda for their cause.

D. The colonists bitterly retreated and followed Britain's laws once more.

**3. What happened at the Boston Tea Party?**

A. The colonial army shot many British soldiers on the docks in Boston.

B. The Sons of Liberty dressed as Mohawk Indians and dumped tea overboard.

C. The colonists brewed homegrown tea and had a party in Boston Square.

D. The British tarred and feathered colonists and tried to make them drink tea.

**4. What events led to the battles of Lexington and Concord?**

A. The Intolerable Acts weren't repealed, so colonists began collecting weapons.

B. Colonial spies organized an army and attacked General Gage and his troops.

C. To protest taxes, the colonial army fought some British soldiers and won.

D. The British attacked Concord to make them pay their taxes.

**5. Which is true about the Battle of Concord?**

A. Paul Revere met the colonial army at Concord and informed them that it was time to fight.

B. The British tried to seize the colonists' weapons but ran into the Minutemen.

C. General Gage led his army to Concord and overtook the Old North Church.

D. The colonists were ready for the British, but didn't fight because the British retreated.

Name _____     Date _____

6. **Who were the *Minutemen*?**
   A. British soldiers who decided to join the colonists to fight for their cause
   B. a group of colonial soldiers who had only a minute's training before fighting
   C. members of the colonial army who were ready to fight at a minute's notice
   D. a group of very young soldiers who were spies for the British

7. **How did the Battle of Bunker Hill bring the colonies closer to independence?**
   A. It made them realize they needed more supplies, which they began to manufacture.
   B. It gave them hope of being capable of defeating the British.
   C. Many colonists moved to Boston after this battle to help fight the war.
   D. The British were now scared, and many of their troops returned to Britain.

8. **How did *Common Sense* contribute to the movement for independence?**
   A. It convinced many colonists that it was time for them to be free of British rule.
   B. Colonists realized that they had to decide whether or not to stay in America.
   C. Many colonists decided to work secretly for Britain after reading this pamphlet.
   D. It encouraged colonists to form armies and attack the British troops.

9. **What is a *declaration*?**
   A. information used to win support for a cause
   B. a long political speech
   C. a statement or formal announcement
   D. a person chosen to represent a group of people

10. **Why is the Declaration of Independence important to Americans?**
    A. It ended the American Revolution.
    B. It led to freedom of British rule and put into words the American belief in liberty and equality.
    C. It was the first time anyone had formed an organized group in America, and organization is an American ideal.
    D. The signing of this document made people realize the importance of reading and writing to our nation.

Name _____    Date _____

Comprehension Skill: Making Decisions

# Fighting the Revolution

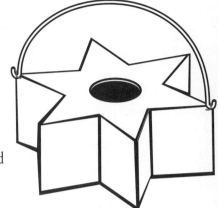

In your textbook you read about important **decisions** that people
have made. Think about their **reasons** for those decisions and the
**effects** of those decisions. Ask yourself, "What might have happened
if different decisions had been made?"

**1–4.**  **Think about what you have already learned. Then reread page 281 before
answering the questions in the chart below.**

| Questions | Answers |
|---|---|
| Why did some colonists decide to remain loyal to the British? | |
| Why did some African Americans decide to become Patriot soldiers? | |
| Why did most Native Americans decide to fight for the British? | |
| Why did two-fifths of the colonists decide not to choose sides at all? | |

**5.**  **Think about what you have learned in Lesson 3 about people's decisions.
How might things have turned out if all of the colonists who chose to stay
out of the war had decided to fight for the British instead?**

_____

_____

Name _____ Date _____

# Fighting the Revolution

Review pages 279-283 to answer these questions. Choose the best answer. Circle the letter next to your choice.

1. **Which of the following was an important strength of the Patriot side during the War for Independence?**
   A. Their generals were very experienced.
   B. They had better weapons than the British.
   C. They felt enthusiasm for their cause.
   D. They were able to hire mercenaries.

2. **Which of the following was an important strength of the British side during the War for Independence?**
   A. British fighting methods worked well on American soil.
   B. They could get all the supplies they needed in America.
   C. The British were dedicated to fighting for their country.
   D. Most Native Americans supported the British.

3. **What is a *mercenary*?**
   A. a paid soldier
   B. someone who is greedy for money
   C. one who sells guns and other weapons
   D. a trainer of soldiers

4. **What is a *revolution*?**
   A. an attempt to overthrow one government and replace it with another
   B. when a soldier from one side deserted to the other side
   C. the invasion of land for the purpose of expanding one's territory
   D. fighting for one's ideals

5. **Which was a weakness of the Continental Army?**
   A. They had no other European countries on their side.
   B. They were untrained beginners.
   C. They weren't used to fighting in the same way as the British.
   D. They had to get their weapons and supplies from across the sea.

Name _____ Date _____

## Maps from Written Descriptions

# Map It Yourself

Read this description to learn how Patriot troops were able to defeat General Burgoyne at Saratoga in 1777.

The British plan had three major parts. General Burgoyne was to travel south from Canada, down Lake Champlain and the Hudson River. Colonel St. Leger was to travel east from Oswego through the Mohawk River Valley. Sir William Howe was to travel north up the Hudson River from New York City. All three leaders were to meet victorious in Albany.

St. Leger started eastward and attacked Fort Stanwix. His troops were tricked by American General Benedict Arnold and forced to retreat back to Oswego.

Rather than traveling north, Howe changed plans and tried to capture Philadelphia.

Burgoyne followed the original plan. However, when he and his troops battled Patriot forces at Saratoga, no British troops came from the west or south to aid him. Burgoyne was forced to surrender.

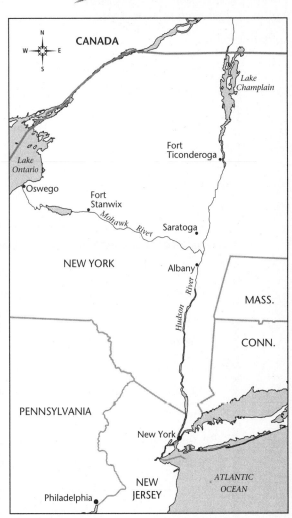

1. **In the box, make a legend using a different color for the routes of each of the three British leaders.**

   **Use solid lines** ——— **to show their planned routes.**

   **Use dotted lines** - - - - - - - **to show their actual routes.**

2. **Using the colors in your legend, draw the planned and actual routes on the map.**

Name _____     Date _____

## Maps from Written Descriptions

# The National Mall

The National Mall is a long, rectangular grassy area in Washington, D.C. Read this description of some of the sites found on the Mall, and draw a map in the space below. Label each site after you draw it on the map.  The Reflecting Pool has been added for you.

N
W &#9670; E
S

**Reflecting
Pool**

The Lincoln Memorial is located at the far west end of the Mall, facing the Reflecting Pool.  It houses a huge marble statue of Abraham Lincoln.

At the other end of the Reflecting Pool is a large, grassy area.  In the center of this area is the Washington Monument.  The monument is the tallest structure in the city.

Located at the east end of the mall, facing the Washington Monument, is the U.S. Capitol.  In this building, members of Congress write the laws for our country.

About halfway down the Mall on the north side is the National Museum of American History.  Many historic items are found there, such as the flag that inspired "The Star-Spangled Banner."

Just east of that museum is the National Museum of Natural History. The National Gallery of Art is located between the National Museum of Natural History and the Capitol.

Across from the National Gallery of Art on the south side of the Mall is the National Air and Space Museum. There you can touch a rock brought back by Apollo astronauts when they visited the Moon.

Skills Workshop

Name _____ Date _____

Comprehension Skill: Understanding Text Organization–General

# Winning the Revolution

Good writers **organize** their writing so that readers can understand it. Recognizing how information in your textbook is organized helps you understand each lesson.

**The authors of your textbook sometimes organize facts by describing *causes* and *effects*. Reread these passages and complete the cause-effect charts:**

1. **Page 286:**

**Causes:**

_____

_____

**Effect:** *Nearly one-quarter of the soldiers at Valley Forge died.*

2. **First two paragraphs on page 287:**

**Causes:**

Benjamin Franklin went to Paris to ask the French for help.

_____

**Effect:** *France entered the Revolutionary War on the Patriot side.*

3. **Which is the best description of the way this lesson is organized? Circle the letter next to the correct answer.**

A. *All* of the events described in the lesson are listed in sequence. Each section tells about a different time period.

B. *Most* of the events described are told in sequence. Some sections describe reasons why the Patriots eventually won. Some sections tell how the war was fought in different regions.

C. *Few* of the events are described in sequence. Each section tells about a different European country that helped the Patriots.

Name _____ Date _____

# Winning the Revolution

Review pages 286-291 to answer these questions. Choose the best answer. Circle the letter next to your choice.

1. **Which was NOT a way European nations helped the Continental Army?**
   A. by sending generals to train the Continental Army
   B. by giving them supplies
   C. by providing them with well-trained troops
   D. by donating money

2. **What does *intervention* mean?**
   A. when one nation enters the affairs of another nation
   B. when someone teaches a skill to someone inexperienced
   C. when one event makes another event happen
   D. a meeting of representatives to accomplish a specific goal

3. **What does *neutral* mean?**
   A. when someone is forced into a military system
   B. the killing of many people
   C. belonging to the American colonies, but being loyal to Britain
   D. choosing to stay out of a war

4. **Where did Francis Marion, "the Swamp Fox," and his men fight?**
   A. in New Orleans
   B. at Fort Vincennes on the Wabash River
   C. in the South Carolina low country
   D. in Baton Rouge

5. **Where did the British troops surrender?**
   A. Boston
   B. Yorktown
   C. Concord
   D. Lexington

Lesson Review

Name _____ Date _____

Comprehension Skill: Making Predictions

# The Impact of the Revolution

Making a **prediction** about what you might learn in a lesson or a chapter can help you understand what you read. A **preview,** or a quick look ahead, at what you will read can help you make predictions.

1.  Preview Lesson 3. Read the title and the Main Idea sentence at the top of page 294. Read the headings and Focus questions and look at the map and illustrations in the lesson. What will you learn about in this lesson? Circle the letter next to the prediction that seems most complete.

    A.  I will learn how France helped the Patriots win the war.

    B.  I will learn about the lives of Native Americans after the war.

    C.  I will learn how the war changed Americans' lives.

2.  Look at the map and read the caption on page 294. Read the heading and the Focus question on page 295. Also look at the illustration and read the caption on this page. What will you learn about in this section? Answer with a complete sentence.

    Prediction: _____

    _____

3.  Preview the section titled "The War Changes America" on pages 296–297, including the special feature called "Ask Yourself." Predict what you will learn about in this section.

    Prediction: _____

    _____

4.  Read the lesson. Check your predictions after you have finished reading. How close were your predictions to what you read?

    _____

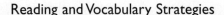

Reading and Vocabulary Strategies

Name _____  Date _____

# The Impact of the Revolution

Review pages 294-297 to answer these questions. Choose the best answer. Circle the letter next to your choice.

1. **What is a *diplomat*?**
   A. someone who sails from one country to another
   B. a government's representative who deals with other nations
   C. a person who agrees with someone else
   D. one who sets boundaries for nations

2. **What does *negotiate* mean?**
   A. to become a new citizen of a nation
   B. to recognize independence
   C. to talk over issues and try to reach an agreement
   D. to return to one's home country

3. **The Treaty of Paris stated that—**
   A. the war had officially ended
   B. all of North America was free of British rule
   C. France would help rebuild America
   D. Spain and France would help America structure their new government

4. **How did the Treaty of Paris change the map of North America?**
   A. All of Canada now became part of colonial America.
   B. The southern states no longer belonged to Spain but were part of the U.S.
   C. Land west of the Rocky Mountains now belonged to the colonists, too.
   D. The western U.S. border reached the Mississippi River and Spain kept its land.

5. **Which was NOT an effect the Revolution had on the lives of Americans?**
   A. Loyalists fled the country.
   B. Native Americans were given new rights.
   C. Many people died.
   D. Some enslaved people were freed.

Lesson Review

Name _____ Date _____

# The War for Independence

Review pages 278-299 to answer these questions. Choose the best answer. Circle the letter next to your choice.

1. **What were the British goals in the early part of the war?**
   A. to bring as many troops as possible from Britain to fight the war quickly
   B. to stop rebellion before France and Spain joined the Patriots
   C. to attack the colonists and get rid of their ideas of independence
   D. to capture all the Patriot generals and make them surrender

2. **George Washington's strategy in the early part of the war was to—**
   A. fight when he had to and then retreat
   B. get mercenaries to join the cause for freedom
   C. show the British how large and strong his army was
   D. trick the British into fighting the war in the South

3. **How did the French help to change the war?**
   A. They sent their army and navy to Britain to fight the war there.
   B. They attacked the British by surprise at Concord and entered the war.
   C. French generals met with British generals to join forces against the Patriots.
   D. They provided experienced officers and troops to aid the Continental Army.

4. **Who was George Rogers Clark?**
   A. a professional soldier from Prussia who trained the Patriot troops
   B. a soldier who captured three forts, forcing the British to surrender
   C. a soldier who led troops through southern swamps to attack the British
   D. a friend of Washington who was put in charge of military supplies

5. **How did events in the West help the Patriots' cause?**
   A. Settlers from the West Coast returned home to help the Patriots fight.
   B. Native Americans in the West joined the Continental Army.
   C. Clark's victories and aid from Spanish Governor Galvez boosted the Patriot army.
   D. Gun factories were built in the West to supply Patriots with weapons.

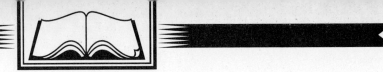

Name _____  Date _____

6. **Why did the British want to move the war to the South?**

   A.  They thought it would be a better climate to fight in during the winter.

   B.  The landscape in the South was more like what they were used to in Britain.

   C.  They hoped the French troops could not find them in the South.

   D.  They thought this region was full of Loyalists ready to battle for the British.

7. **How did the Revolution affect Native Americans?**

   A.  They joined with the Patriots at the peace talks and rebuilt their homes.

   B.  They were encouraged to vote and be part of the new America.

   C.  The new government took away much of their land.

   D.  all of the above

8. **After the Revolution, how did some African Americans begin to stand up for their rights?**

   A.  They created their own churches.

   B.  Many convinced the southern plantation owners to free them.

   C.  They wrote to Washington, D.C., for freedom and were given special papers.

   D.  Many became lawyers and fought for the rights of their people.

9. **Why did the United States and France make separate peace treaties with Britain?**

   A.  French leaders were still in the U.S., so the two countries negotiated together.

   B.  Britain requested that the peace treaties be structured this way.

   C.  The United States and France worked together for unity.

   D.  The Americans did not totally trust the French.

10. **What happened to the Loyalists after the Revolution?**

   A.  Many Loyalists fled to Canada.

   B.  Many Loyalists were forced to give up their possessions and return to Britain.

   C.  Many Loyalists were thrown in jail in America.

   D.  Many Loyalists moved to Spain and France.

Name _____ Date _____

Comprehension Skill: Understanding Cause and Effect

# The Government in Trouble

You have learned that a **cause** is an event or condition that makes something else happen. What happens as a result of the cause is its **effect**.

**I.  In the sentence below, underline the cause once and the effect twice.**

Without a strong national government, the states began to act like 13 different countries.

Reread page 306, then read the pairs of sentences below. Write C in front of the sentence that describes a cause and E in front of the sentence that describes its effect.

**2.  ____  The men in Washington's army had empty stomachs and ragged uniforms.**

**____  Congress couldn't raise enough money to support the army.**

**3.  ____  Colonists remembered how Parliament had "meddled in their affairs."**

**____  Colonists did not want to give Congress much power.**

Sometimes one event causes a second event, the second event causes a third event, and so on. This is a **cause-effect chain**. Reread pages 308-309. Then complete the chain below.

**4.  What was the cause of Shays' Rebellion? Write your answer in the first Cause box of the cause-effect chain.**

**5-6.  Finish the sentence in the third box. Then fill in the last box in the chain.**

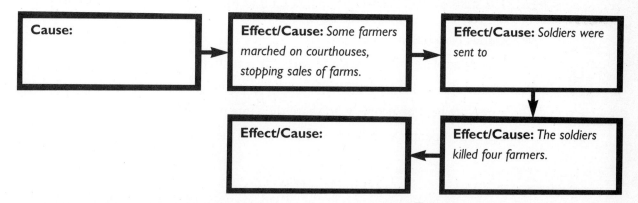

Reading and Vocabulary Strategies

Name _____ Date _____

# The Government in Trouble

Review pages 305-309 to answer these questions. Choose the best answer. Circle the letter next to your choice.

1. **What is a *constitution*?**
   A. a large group of people who work together
   B. money that is raised by taxes on goods
   C. a written plan of how a government works
   D. an area of land ruled by a government

2. **How did Congress settle the disputes over the Northwest Territory?**
   A. Congress allowed this new land to be claimed by several states.
   B. Congress set up state banks and issued special paper money.
   C. Congress gave people new jobs on the nearby lakes and rivers.
   D. Congress established rules about how to divide the land into new states.

3. **Name three states in what was called the Northwest Territory.**
   A. Ohio, Kentucky, and Virginia
   B. Michigan, Ohio, and Wisconsin
   C. Indiana, Illinois, and Tennessee
   D. Iowa, West Virginia, and Ohio

4. **What was the cause of Shays' Rebellion?**
   A. Farmers couldn't pay their taxes and lost their farms.
   B. There was a long hard winter and crops were poor.
   C. Farmers wanted to be in the army to fight again.
   D. The state wanted farmers to donate food to the poor.

5. **What does *convention* mean?**
   A. a meeting place where laws and rules are rewritten
   B. a large area of land ruled by a common government
   C. a meeting held by people who share the same purpose
   D. a group of people who borrowed money for the war

Lesson Review

Name _____ Date _____

Comprehension Strategy: SQ3R

# Something New Under the Sun

The **SQ3R strategy** can help you understand and remember the information in textbook lessons. Here are the steps of SQ3R:

**S:** **Survey** the lesson or chapter. Read the main headings and the subheadings. Look at the illustrations and read the captions.

**Q:** Make each heading and subheading into a **question.**

**R:** **Read** the lesson to find the answers to those questions.

**R:** **Recite** (say aloud) and **write** answers to your questions.

**R:** **Review** the lesson by rereading your questions and answers.

Follow the steps of SQ3R and complete the chart below as you read Lesson 2. You can write the Focus questions or think of your own questions.

| Before Reading (Survey and Question) | After Reading (Recite and Write Answers) |
|---|---|
| page 310<br><br>**1.** Title: Something New Under the Sun<br><br>**2.** Your question: Why was a new<br><br>government needed? | **7.** |
| page 311<br><br>**3.** Heading: Madison's Plan<br><br>**4.** Your question: _____<br><br>_____ | **8.** |
| page 312–313<br><br>**5.** Subheading: _____<br><br>**6.** Your question: _____<br><br>_____ | **9.** |

Name _____  Date _____

# Something New Under the Sun

Review pages 310-316 to answer these questions. Choose the best answer. Circle the letter next to your choice.

1. **How did James Madison come up with a plan for a strong national government?**
   A. by asking George Washington for help with this plan
   B. by working with Roger Sherman to write the Constitution
   C. by meeting with government leaders from Great Britain for advice
   D. by studying the strengths and weaknesses of earlier democratic governments

2. **What is a *republic*?**
   A. a government in which citizens elect representatives
   B. a place where the government meets to make decisions about laws
   C. division of power between many branches of government
   D. an equal number of votes for each state

3. **Why were many delegates late to the Constitutional Convention?**
   A. They were fighting in the war.
   B. Mail was very slow, and some got their invitations late.
   C. Spring rains turned many roads to mud.
   D. There was a late snowstorm that blocked many roads.

4. **What is a *compromise*?**
   A. a fight over power
   B. a document signed by many
   C. someone who votes for an issue
   D. an agreement

5. **The Antifederalists wanted—**
   A. the states to have more power
   B. the President to have all the power
   C. the towns to control the government
   D. to sign the Constitution

Lesson Review

Name _____    Date _____

Using Organizational Charts

# Who's in Charge?

Study this organizational chart of the executive branch.

| The Executive Branch of Government |
| --- |

| President |
| --- |

| **Executive Office** | **Executive Departments** | **Independent Agencies** |
| --- | --- | --- |
| Includes: | Includes: | Includes: |
| Office of Management and Budget | Defense Department | Environmental Protection Agency |
| White House Office | Education Department | United States Postal Service |

Complete the following activities.

1.  **Who is in charge of the Executive Office, the Executive Departments, and the Independent Agencies?** _____

2.  **The Department of Education is headed by the Secretary of Education. That person reports to the President. Several people report to the Secretary — a deputy secretary, a general counsel, an inspector general, and several assistant secretaries. Create an organizational chart for the Department of Education in the space below. Put the President at the top of your chart.**

Name _____  Date _____

Using Organizational Charts

# Earth Colony – A.D. 2776

The year is A.D. 2776. You need to set up an executive branch of government for the colony on planet Zewok.

1. What will the leader of the colony be called?

   _____

2. What are three departments he or she will supervise?

   A. _____

   B. _____

   C. _____

3. Each of the departments in question 2 will have a smaller department under it. List the smaller departments' names.

   A. _____

   B. _____

   C. _____

4. In the space below, create an organizational chart that summarizes the colony's executive branch.

Name _____ Date _____

Study Skill: Taking Notes

# Our Federal Government

**Taking notes** can help you remember the information you read in your textbook. Here are some reminders about note taking:

• Use the headings and subheadings to help identify the topic of each section.

• Note the topic and main ideas of each section and the most important details. The Main Idea sentences and Focus questions in the textbook help identify main ideas.

• Don't try to write complete sentences. Just jot down key points.

**1-4.** **Lesson 3 describes how the federal government is organized. As you read the lesson, use the chart below to take notes. Include information from the charts, diagrams, and captions.**

| Lesson Sections | Notes |
|---|---|
| Introduction, page 318 | |
| "Sharing Power," page 319 | |
| "A System of Checks and Balances," pages 319–320 | |
| "Changing the Constitution," pages 320–321 | |

Name _____ Date _____

# Our Federal Government

Review pages 318-321 to answer these questions. Choose the best answer. Circle the letter next to your choice.

1.  **How does the Constitution separate powers within the federal government?**
    A.  Each state has an equal vote within the federal government.
    B.  The Senate and House of Representatives can never meet together.
    C.  Congress makes laws, the President carries out the laws, and the Supreme Court settles arguments about the meaning of laws.
    D.  The Constitution tells who can vote.

2.  **Which branch is headed by the Supreme Court?**
    A.  the executive branch
    B.  the judicial branch
    C.  the legislative branch
    D.  the military branch

3.  **What must happen for an amendment to take effect?**
    A.  Three-quarters of the states must approve it.
    B.  The President must write the amendment.
    C.  The Supreme Court must suggest the amendment take effect.
    D.  Each branch of the government must agree on the amendment.

4.  **What is the importance of the Bill of Rights?**
    A.  It doesn't protect the rights of some people.
    B.  It puts an end to slavery.
    C.  It allows the majority to rule.
    D.  It protects the rights of individuals.

5.  **Which of the following powers belongs to the states?**
    A.  declare war
    B.  print money
    C.  establish schools
    D.  organize military

Name _____ Date _____

## Comprehension Skill: Comparing and Contrasting

# A New Beginning

You have learned to **compare** and **contrast** two things or two people by thinking about the ways they are similar and the ways they are different.

**1-5.** Reread the section called "Two Views of the Future" on pages 323-325. Also read the special feature called "Tell Me More" on page 323. Use the chart below to take notes.

|  | Thomas Jefferson, Secretary of State | Alexander Hamilton, Secretary of the Treasury |
|---|---|---|
| What were each man's cabinet responsibilities? | | |
| How did each man feel about repaying the debt from the Revolutionary War? | | |
| How did each man feel about establishing a national bank? | | |
| How much power did each man want to give to the people to rule themselves? | | |
| What political party did each man form? | | |

Name _____ Date _____

# A New Beginning

Review pages 322-325 to answer these questions. Choose the best answer. Circle the letter next to your choice.

1.  **In which city was George Washington sworn in as the first President?**

    A.  Mount Vernon

    B.  Washington, D.C.

    C.  New York City

    D.  Philadelphia

2.  **What is a *precedent*?**

    A.  a special name for the President

    B.  a past decision used as a model for a later decision

    C.  a view that is different from that of the President's

    D.  someone who worked for the former government

3.  **What is the President's *cabinet*?**

    A.  the place where the President has meetings

    B.  the President's office

    C.  a weekend home

    D.  a group of advisors

4.  **How did Congress address the President?**

    A.  "His Most Benign Highness"

    B.  "Mr. President"

    C.  "Mr. Washington"

    D.  "George"

5.  **Which of the following was NOT a view of Thomas Jefferson?**

    A.  He trusted ordinary people to rule themselves.

    B.  He pictured a nation of family farms.

    C.  He wanted to establish a national bank.

    D.  He wanted to help the French in their own revolution.

Lesson Review

Name _____ Date _____

# The Constitution

Review pages 304-331 to answer these questions. Choose the best answer. Circle the letter next to your choice.

1. **What was the problem with the Articles of Confederation, passed in 1777?**
   A. People were afraid that the government might tell them exactly what to do.
   B. It gave more power to the states than to the national government.
   C. Settlers in the Northwest Territory and Native Americans didn't get along.
   D. Congress established rules about how to divide and sell land.

2. **Why was the ban on slavery in the Northwest Territory important?**
   A. No one realized that this was an important rule at the time.
   B. It became the model for settling all future territories.
   C. It caused settlers to sign a peace treaty and live safely.
   D. It was soon known as the Northwest Ordinance of 1787.

3. **What was the effect of Shays' Rebellion?**
   A. George Washington told the farmers to return home.
   B. Farmers left their land and never paid taxes again.
   C. Daniel Shays was killed in a battle in Massachusetts.
   D. People realized the need to strengthen the national government.

4. **What was the purpose of the convention in Philadelphia in May of 1787?**
   A. to establish a fair and equal system of taxation for farmers
   B. to send representatives to settle the Northwest Territory
   C. to end Shays' Rebellion and help the farmers start over
   D. to rewrite and strengthen the Articles of Confederation

5. **How did the delegates to the Constitutional Convention settle their differences?**
   A. by giving all the power to the federal government
   B. by giving all the power to the states
   C. by each side giving up something it wanted
   D. by dividing all the power among the people, enslaved or not, in the states

Name _____ Date _____

6. **How was the Constitution approved by the states?**

   A. After the delegates read the Constitution, each signed it to show his state's approval.

   B. The Constitution was taken from state to state and voted on by the people.

   C. The Federalists promised to add a bill of rights, and the Constitution was then approved by all 13 states.

   D. Three-fourths of U.S. citizens voted and approved the Constitution.

7. **How does the Constitution divide power between the states and the federal government?**

   A. Equal power is given to state governments and the federal government.

   B. Most power is the states'. A few issues are decided by the federal government.

   C. The federal government tells state governments what to do.

   D. States control local issues, and the federal government controls national issues.

8. **What are *checks and balances*?**

   A. the system of balancing power between the three branches of government

   B. the money spent to operate government

   C. the way that taxes are divided to support different states

   D. the balancing of the President's budget

9. **Which of these best describes Hamilton's ideas about the U.S. and its government?**

   A. The United States should be a nation of farms and small industries in large cities. The government should control these.

   B. The United States should help the French, since the French helped them in the fight against Britain. Governments should work together.

   C. Revolutionary War loans shouldn't be repaid. The people should run government.

   D. The U.S. needed a strong national government of rich and powerful men.

10. **What advice did Washington give the country before he retired?**

   A. avoid permanent alliances with other countries

   B. form two political parties to give people choices

   C. name the capital city after himself

   D. to not allow Presidents to hold office for a third term

Chapter Review

Name _____    Date _____

Comprehension Skill: Understanding Sequence of Events

# The Age of Jefferson

When you read about historical events, it is important to understand the **sequence of events,** or the order in which events happened. **Dates** and **time-order words** such as *first, later,* and *finally,* help you figure out the correct sequence of events.

1. **The events listed below are out of order. Review the section called "The Lewis and Clark Expedition" on pages 338-339. Then write a number on the line in front of each sentence to show the correct order.**

   _3_ The Lewis and Clark expedition moved up the Missouri River.

   _6_ The Corps reached the Pacific Ocean.

   _7_ The expedition headed home.

   _4_ A French trader and his Shoshone wife joined Lewis and Clark as interpreters.

   _2_ Lewis and Clark and about 40 others left St. Louis in May, 1804.

   _5_ The Corps spent the winter at Fort Clatsop.

   _1_ President Thomas Jefferson chose Meriwether Lewis to lead the Corps of Discovery.

2. **Write a paragraph that describes the Lewis and Clark expedition. Use dates and time-order words to make the sequence clear.**

   _____

   _____

   _____

   _____

   _____

Name _____ Date _____

# The Age of Jefferson

Review pages 335-339 to answer these questions. Choose the best answer. Circle the letter next to your choice.

1.  **Which of these best describes Thomas Jefferson?**
    A.  a bold leader who met with Tecumseh to discuss Native Americans
    B.  a farmer, an inventor, and the third U.S. President
    C.  an author of the Constitution
    D.  a painter, a leader of pioneers, and a master gardener

2.  **What is a *frontier*?**
    A.  a long path leading to a new settlement
    B.  a group of people who move west to a new land
    C.  a region just beyond, or at the edge of, a settled area
    D.  a space between two mountains

3.  **Who was Daniel Boone?**
    A.  a representative who bought New Orleans
    B.  a soldier who died in the Battle of Tippecanoe
    C.  a frontiersman who moved to Kentucky
    D.  the founder of the Federalist party

4.  **What doubled the size of the U.S.?**
    A.  the Spanish Possession
    B.  the settlement of Boonesborough
    C.  the Cumberland Gap
    D.  the Louisiana Purchase

5.  **What did Lewis and Clark do?**
    A.  found a river that was a shortcut to the Pacific Ocean
    B.  led pioneers on the Wilderness Trail across the U.S.
    C.  learned about the land, plants, animals, and plants of the West
    D.  designed buildings, trained horses, and studied the stars

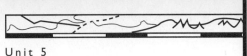

Name _____ Date _____

*Places and Regions*

# How Did Lewis and Clark Learn About the West?

Lewis and Clark traveled west of the Mississippi River to gather geographic and other scientific information.

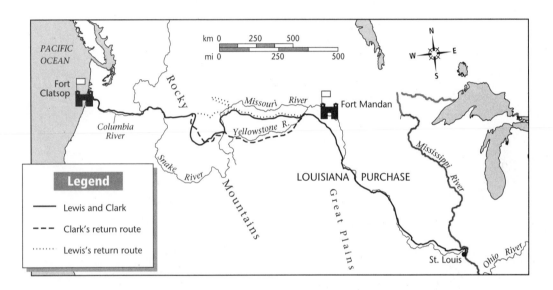

Use the map above to answer the following questions. Write your answers on the map and below.

1. **President Jefferson hoped that Lewis and Clark would find a direct water route to the Pacific Ocean. Many scientists at the time believed the Mississippi, Missouri, and Columbia Rivers were one continuous waterway. Which one actually empties into the Pacific Ocean?** _____

2. **About how many miles in all did Meriwether Lewis travel?** _____

3. **Why do you think the expedition spent the winter of 1804-1805 at Fort Mandan?**

   _____

   _____

   _____

Think Like a Geographer

Name _____ Date _____

# A Growing America

Use the map above to answer the following questions.

1. **Color in the area of the Louisiana Purchase. What present-day states are made from it?**

   _____

   _____

2. **Pencil in Lewis and Clark's route. Near what present-day cities did they travel?**

   _____

Name _____ Date _____

## Comprehension Strategy: Summarizing a Lesson

# The War of 1812

When you **summarize** text, you briefly retell the most important ideas in your own words. Use the following procedure to summarize Lesson 2:

**Step 1:** After you have read the lesson once, scan the text again. Write the **topic** of Lesson 2 in the box below.

> **Topic:**

**Step 2: Reread** any parts of Lesson 2 that confused you.

**Step 3:** Find the **main ideas** of the lesson. Some main ideas from pages 346-347 have been written for you. Find two or three more main ideas on pages 347-349 and write them in the box below.

> **Main Ideas:**
>
> • France and Britain were at war with each other. Each attacked United States ships trading with their enemy.
> • Britain captured American sailors and forced them to join the British navy.
> • The British sided with the Shawnee in the Battle of Tippecanoe.
> • The War Hawks wanted to fight to end British support of Native American uprisings and the impressment of American sailors.

**Step 4:** Using a separate sheet of paper, write a **summary** of Lesson 2. In your summary, remember to include only the most important information in the lesson.

Name _____     Date _____

# The War of 1812

Review pages 346-349 to answer these questions. Choose the best answer. Circle the letter next to your choice.

1. **Why did the United States go to war with Britain?**
   A. to help the Native Americans keep their land
   B. to increase trade with France and other European nations
   C. to end British support of Native American uprisings
   D. to stop the British from trading with Canada

2. **What is *impressment*?**
   A. to attack a ship in foreign waters
   B. to force people into military service
   C. to work to unite Native American people
   D. to try to win another country's favor

3. **What happened at the Battle of Tippecanoe?**
   A. Governor Harrison led an army against the Shawnee.
   B. Many canoes were overturned in the cold, icy river.
   C. Americans fought French and German troops in the woods.
   D. The British secretly attacked the Americans at night.

4. **What did Tecumseh want?**
   A. to move to Britain to start a settlement
   B. to lead the largest, most powerful group of Native Americans
   C. to unite all midwestern Native American groups as one
   D. to share the Native Americans' land with Britain and America

5. **What was the result of the War of 1812?**
   A. The British won the war, but Americans were not defeated.
   B. Neither side won, but American unity increased.
   C. America lost the war, but quickly began another one.
   D. The British and Americans became friends.

Name _____ Date _____

## Study Skill: Examining Visuals as Part of Previewing

# Becoming American

**Visuals** are the illustrations, photographs, maps, charts, and diagrams included in your textbook. When you preview a chapter or a lesson, look at each visual and think about what it shows.

Look at the visuals on pages 354-355. Read the captions, too. What do you see in each one? Write your descriptions below.

1. painting on page 354: _____

2. drawing on page 355: _____

3. photographs on page 355: _____

4. What do you think you will read about on these two pages?

   _____

5-7. A symbol is something that represents something else. The "Tell Me More" feature on page 355 discusses the eagle and two other symbols. Using the information in the special feature, fill in the chart below.

| Symbol | What the symbol stands for |
|---|---|
| eagle | |
| arrows in the eagle's claw | |
| olive branch in the eagle's claw | |

Name _____  Date _____

# Becoming American

Review pages 354-358 to answer these questions. Choose the best answer. Circle the letter next to your choice.

1. **What is a *hero*?**
   A. a person known for a special achievement
   B. someone who is killed in a war
   C. someone who writes American literature
   D. one who designs patriotic symbols

2. **Which is NOT an example of an American symbol?**
   A. the Liberty Bell
   B. the American flag
   C. Miss Liberty
   D. the Continental Congress

3. **What bird did Benjamin Franklin choose for the national bird?**
   A. the chicken
   B. the eagle
   C. the wild turkey
   D. the parrot

4. **Why did Franklin choose this national bird?**
   A. because it was only found in North America
   B. because it has been a symbol of power for hundreds of years
   C. because most Americans prefer this bird
   D. because it is such a colorful bird

5. **What do the stripes on the American flag represent?**
   A. the thirteen original states
   B. the number of amendments to the Constitution
   C. the number of people who signed the Declaration of Independence
   D. the thirteen ships which first came to America

Name _____     Date _____

Organizing and Recording Information

# Word for Word

| The Incredible Journey of Lewis and Clark |
|---|
| Rhoda Blumberg |
| Lothrop, Lee & Shepard, 1987, p. 76 |
| "among the most happy in my life" |
| A description of how Lewis felt at the point when they were beginning their journey into unknown parts |
| (April, 1805) |

| In the Footsteps of Lewis and Clark |
|---|
| Gerald S. Snyder |
| National Geographic Society, 1970, p.195 |
| "In obedience to your orders we have penitrated the continent of North America to the Pacific Ocean, and sufficiently explored the interior of the country to affirm with confidence that we have discovered the most practicable rout which dose exist across the continent." |
| From a letter at the end of the journey from Lewis to Thomas Jefferson (September, 1806) |

Read the note cards about Lewis and Clark's journey. Since they are direct quotations, any misspelled words match the spelling of the explorers.

1. **Think about the quotation on the first card. Why might you want to include it in a report about Lewis and Clark? Explain.**

   _____

   _____

   _____

2. **Underline what you think are the most important parts of the quote on the second card. Then rewrite the quote in your own words.**

   _____

   _____

   _____

   _____

   _____

Name _____   Date _____

Organizing and Recording Information

# Who Said It?

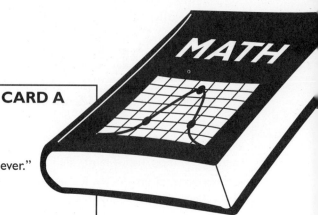

**A. My Soul Looks Back, 'Less I Forget**                    **CARD A**

Dorothy Winbush Riley, editor

HarperCollins, 1993, p.110

"One's work may be finished some day, but one's education never."

Alexandre Dumas, about 1856

**B. My Soul Looks Back, 'Less I Forget**                    **CARD B**

Dorothy Winbush Riley, editor

HarperCollins, 1993, p.111

"Education is a ladder."

**C.**                                                       **CARD C**

"Education is the key to unlock the golden door of freedom."

George Washington Carver, about 1912

Read the notecards and then complete the following activities.

1.  **Read the quotation by Dumas on Card A. Paraphrase it, or rewrite it in your own words, at the bottom of the card.**

2.  **The quotation on Card B comes from a speech given to Congress in 1865 by Manuelito of the Navahos. Write the information about the speaker at the bottom of the card.**

3.  **The quotation on Card C was found on the same page as the one on Card B. Write the information needed to credit the source.**

Name _____     Date _____

# The Early Republic

Review pages 334-361 to answer these questions. Choose the best answer. Circle the letter next to your choice.

1.  **What is a *corps*?**
    A.  a plot of land settled by pioneers
    B.  an organized group of people
    C.  a map used to travel west
    D.  a river used for transportation

2.  **Where did the Wilderness Trail lead?**
    A.  from the Mississippi to the Ohio River
    B.  from eastern Virginia to the Kentucky River
    C.  from Florida to New Orleans
    D.  from the Snake River to the Pacific Ocean

3.  **What was the role of pioneers in settling the frontier?**
    A.  to become friends with the Native Americans who lived there
    B.  to build roads and guide other settlers to the area
    C.  to secure more land for the United States
    D.  to move west to build homes and work the land

4.  **Why did Thomas Jefferson want the land the Mississippi River flowed through?**
    A.  He thought Napoleon might keep Americans from using the Mississippi River.
    B.  He knew the land was very expensive.
    C.  He wanted people to be able to fish in the river for free.
    D.  There were too many people living in the U.S., and it was overcrowded.

5.  **Which is NOT a place where the War of 1812 was fought?**
    A.  in the western territories
    B.  in Texas
    C.  along the border of the U.S. and Canada
    D.  along the Atlantic coastline

6. **Who was known as "Old Hickory"?**

   A. Andrew Jackson

   B. George Washington

   C. Captain James Lawrence

   D. Henry Clay

7. **Who was Dolley Madison?**

   A. the head librarian at the national library in Washington, D.C.

   B. a British woman who wanted peace for her country

   C. an American who helped women get involved with the war effort

   D. the First Lady who saved valuables from the White House

8. **What led to the increase of patriotic heroes and symbols following the War of 1812?**

   A. There was a contest funded by the American government to design new patriotic symbols after the war.

   B. Americans were proud of their young nation.

   C. Many artists had immigrated to America following the War of 1812, and they wanted to show thanks for their new freedom.

   D. During the war many heroes died, so the American government dedicated a memorial to them.

9. **How did changes in language and education make Americans feel more connected to one another?**

   A. All Americans were required to learn to speak American English, which enabled them to read the new literature in schools.

   B. Americans now shared a standardized language, a school system, and new literature about American life.

   C. Students recited their lessons to show that they could speak the new language.

   D. When all Americans were allowed to go to public schools, it showed that the country was united and provided equality for all.

10. **Which was NOT true about schools in the early 1800s?**

    A. Not every child went to school.

    B. Reading, writing, math, and citizenship were taught at school.

    C. Free African American children could go to a private school if they paid.

    D. Students wrote their lessons with pencils and paper.

Name _____    Date _____

Comprehension Strategy: Previewing a Lesson

# Jackson: A New Kind of Politics

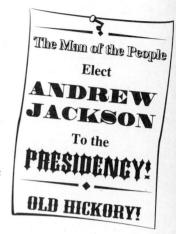

When you **preview** a lesson or chapter, you look ahead at the information in it to find out what you will learn.

Look at the Chapter Preview at the bottom of pages 366–367. This introduces the important people, places, and events you will read about in Chapter 14. Read the titles and captions with the pictures, then answer these questions:

1.  **Which Native American group will you learn about?** _____

2.  **What are the names of two machines that you will learn about?**

    _____

Preview Lesson 1. Read the title, the Main Idea sentence, the headings, the subheading, and the Focus questions. Write the headings and subheading here:

3.  **top of page 368:** _____

4.  **bottom of page 368:** _____

5.  **page 370:** _____

Now look at the visuals in Lesson 1. Describe what each one shows. Two have been described for you:

6.  **page 368:** _____

7.  **page 369:**  <u>a painting by George Caleb Bingham of three men discussing</u>

    <u>politics; an Andrew Jackson election poster.</u>_____

8.  **page 370:** _____

Name _____  Date _____

# Jackson: A New Kind of Politics

Review pages 367-371 to answer these questions. Choose the best answer. Circle the letter next to your choice.

1. **What is *suffrage?***
   A. the right to vote
   B. suffering to make things better
   C. growing up poor
   D. stirring up support for the President

2. **What growing section of the population helped elect Andrew Jackson?**
   A. white women
   B. poor farmers and workers
   C. enslaved Americans
   D. Native Americans

3. **Why did settlers want Congress to pass the Indian Removal Act of 1830?**
   A. Settlers wanted Native Americans to be pioneers in the West.
   B. Settlers were angry with Native Americans and wanted them to move away.
   C. New companies wanted to build mines and railroads in this land.
   D. Settlers wanted the rich land controlled by five Native American nations.

4. **What was the journey of the Native Americans to their new territory called?**
   A. the "Journey Homeland"
   B. the "Trail of Tears"
   C. the "Trail of Mud"
   D. the "Journey West"

5. **What did Sequoya work on for 12 years?**
   A. a plan to free Native Americans from reservations
   B. peace among all Native American groups
   C. the first Cherokee writing system
   D. a new, improved way to grow corn

Name _____ Date _____

## Vocabulary Skill: Technical Terms

# The Industrial Revolution

A **technical term** is a special word or phrase used to discuss a certain topic. For example, *bobbin* and *spinning machines* are technical terms used to discuss the spinning mills.

Review the section called "The Growth of Factories," including the visuals on page 374. Then use the terms below to answer the questions.

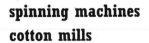

| spinning machines | raw cotton |
|---|---|
| cotton mills | bobbin |

1. **What was cotton called before it became cotton yarn?**

   _____

2. **Making cotton yarn was once a difficult job. What invention made the process easier and faster?**

   _____

3. **What is the name for large buildings where workers made cotton yarn and cloth?**

   _____

4. **What device was used to hold cotton yarn?**

   _____

5. **Write two sentences about cotton mills. Use some of the words and phrases from above.**

   _____

   _____

   _____

Name _____  Date _____

# The Industrial Revolution

Review pages 372-376 to answer these questions. Choose the best answer. Circle the letter next to your choice.

1. **What was the *Industrial Revolution*?**

   A. a time when art, music, and theater became popular

   B. a revolution in farming

   C. a war fought against the use of machines

   D. a time when people started working in factories instead of in their homes

2. **What impact did steamboats, canals, and railroads have on the nation?**

   A. These all caused pollution and harmed the environment.

   B. All of them improved transportation.

   C. More and more scientists moved to the U.S. from other countries.

   D. Rivers were no longer important to the development of cities.

3. **What did Robert Fulton build in 1807?**

   A. a spinning machine that turned raw cotton into cotton

   B. a new canal that helped farmers in Indiana

   C. the first American railroad

   D. a steamboat that was a financial success

4. **What is *mass production*?**

   A. when very large goods are manufactured in a factory

   B. when a large amount of goods is made in a short time

   C. when supplies are produced to be used in churches

   D. when machines make just a few items of one kind which are very valuable

5. **What are *interchangeable parts*?**

   A. parts that are made by man

   B. changes made in factories

   C. parts that change when heated

   D. parts that are identical

Name _____ Date _____

Study Skill: Making an Outline

# North and South: Worlds Apart

**Outlining** a lesson helps you understand and remember the important information in it. To make an outline, write the main topics next to Roman numerals (I, II, III). If there are subtopics, write them next to capital letters (A, B, C). Write important details related to subtopics next to Arabic numerals (1, 2, 3).

This partial outline shows information from the section called "Cotton and Slavery" on pages 378–380. Reread this section. Then complete the outline.

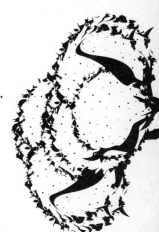

**I. Cotton and Slavery**

    **A. The cotton gin**

        **1. Before the cotton gin, cleaning cotton was a slow process.**

        **2. The cotton gin allowed farmers to plant, process, and sell more cotton.**

        **3. By the mid-1800s, cotton was the most important crop grown in the South.**

    **B. _____**

        **1. As cotton farming boomed, the demand for enslaved workers increased.**

        **2. _____**

        **3. Enslaved African Americans were bought and sold at auctions.**

        **4. _____**

    **C. _____**

        **1. Most white southern families lived on small, self-sufficient farms.**

        **2. _____**

        **3. _____**

Name _____ Date _____

# North and South: Worlds Apart

Review pages 377-382 to answer these questions. Choose the best answer. Circle the letter next to your choice.

1. **What is an *overseer*?**
   A. someone who looks over another person's writing
   B. manager of field workers for plantation owners
   C. one who plants more cotton faster than anyone else
   D. a person who makes predictions about the future

2. **What fear did enslaved people always face?**
   A. working in the fields
   B. starving to death
   C. getting diseases and dying
   D. being separated from their families

3. **What did Nat Turner do?**
   A. invented the cotton gin and interchangeable parts
   B. led a famous slave rebellion in Virginia
   C. found a way to grow more cotton faster
   D. created a new art style in the South

4. **Most southerners lived—**
   A. on farms
   B. in big cities
   C. on large plantations
   D. in ports

5. **When most immigrants arrived, they—**
   A. moved to the South to work on farms
   B. found factory jobs in the North
   C. lived in small towns like the ones they came from
   D. worked in family businesses

Lesson Review

Name _____  Date _____

Comparing Line and Circle Graphs

# Booming Growth

Read and compare these circle and line graphs to learn about
immigration to the United States in the mid 1800s.

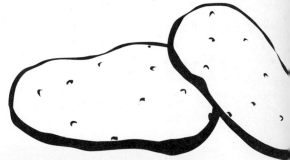

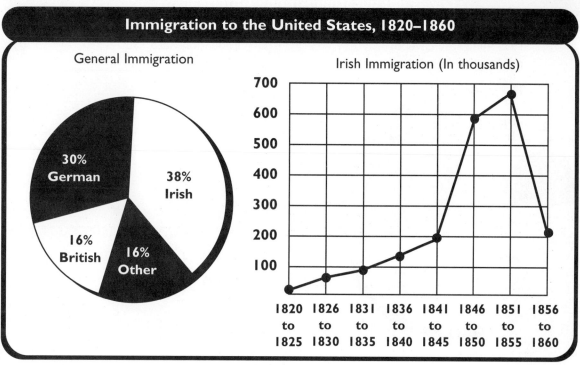

**Immigration to the United States, 1820–1860**

General Immigration

- 30% German
- 38% Irish
- 16% British
- 16% Other

Irish Immigration (In thousands)

700
600
500
400
300
200
100

| 1820 to 1825 | 1826 to 1830 | 1831 to 1835 | 1836 to 1840 | 1841 to 1845 | 1846 to 1850 | 1851 to 1855 | 1856 to 1860 |

Answer the following questions.

1. **During which years did almost 100,000 Irish immigrate to the United States?**

   _____

2. **A diseased potato crop in Ireland caused thousands of people to die of
   hunger and many more to leave. When do you think the Irish potato
   famine happened? Why?**

   _____

   _____

   _____

Name _____ Date _____

Comparing Line and Circle Graphs

# How Many Years of School?

Compare the circle graph and line graph. Each refers to U.S. persons ages 25 and older.

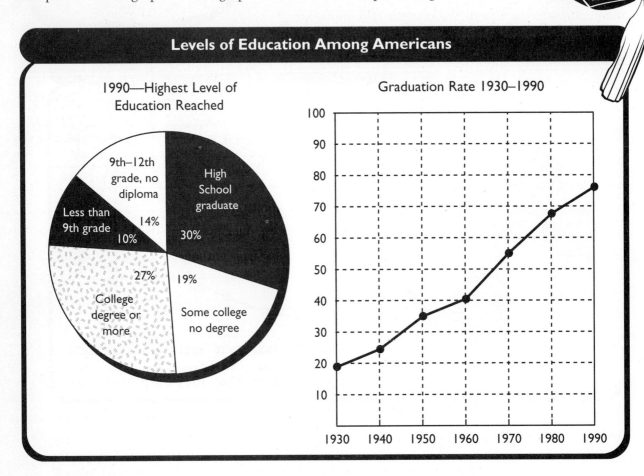

**Levels of Education Among Americans**

1990—Highest Level of Education Reached

Graduation Rate 1930–1990

Complete items 1–2.

1. **In 1930, had most adults finished high school? How do you know?**

    _____

2. **In 1990, what percentage of people ages 25 and older had not graduated from high school? How do you know?**

    _____

Skills Workshop

Name _____ Date _____

Vocabulary Strategy: Structural Analysis

# Spirit of Reform

A **suffix** is a word part that is added to the end of a base word to make a new word. Knowing a suffix and its base word can help you understand unfamiliar terms. Look at the word *conductor*:

>   **conduct** ("to lead or guide") **+**
>   **or** ("one who does a certain thing") **=**
>   **conductor** ("one who leads or guides")

The words in bold type below appear in Lesson 4 (some in slightly different forms). Write the base word and the suffix that make up each word. Next, use the definitions of the suffixes in the box plus the lesson context to write a definition for each word. Finally, check your definitions in a dictionary.

| | |
|---|---|
| **-ist** | "one who performs a special action" |
| **-ity** | "the state of being" |
| **-ly** | "in a way that is" |
| **-er** | "one who does a certain thing" |
| **-ment** | "action or process" |

1.  **(page 384) movement =** _____ **+** _____

    **Movement means** _____

2.  **(page 384) abolitionist =** _____ **+** _____

    **Abolitionist means** _____

3.  **(page 387) equality =** _____ **+** _____

    **Equality means** _____

4.  **(page 388) reformer =** _____ **+** _____

    **Reformer means** _____

5.  **(page 389) supporter =** _____ **+** _____

    **Supporter means** _____

6.  **(page 389) mentally =** _____ **+** _____

    **Mentally means** _____

Name _____ Date _____

# Spirit of Reform

Review pages 384-389 to answer these questions. Choose the best answer. Circle the letter next to your choice.

1. **What was the Second Great Awakening?**
   A. a movement to revive the arts, such as music, painting, and literature
   B. a religious movement that inspired many Americans to join volunteer groups
   C. a call for the North and the South to join together
   D. a newspaper that fought against slavery

2. **How did people work against slavery?**
   A. by speaking out against it in meetings and newspapers
   B. by riding on trains to the South to free slaves
   C. by forming an anti-slavery society
   D. by helping enslaved people to learn how to farm

3. **Who was NOT a leader in the women's right movement?**
   A. Dorothea Dix
   B. Elizabeth Stanton
   C. Susan B. Anthony
   D. Lucretia Mott

4. **What other reform movement had an impact on American life in the 1830s and 1840s?**
   A. reforms to stop gambling
   B. reforms to integrate the schools
   C. reforms to improve education
   D. reforms to improve public health care

5. **What is *temperance*?**
   A. the controlling of one's temper
   B. a law requiring that children go to school at least six months of the year
   C. protection for the mentally ill
   D. when a person does not drink alcohol

Lesson Review

Name _____ Date _____

# People in a Growing Country

Review pages 366-397 to answer these questions. Choose the best answer. Circle the letter next to your choice.

1. **How did the growth of democracy in the United States help Andrew Jackson?**
   A. Jackson was a hero, so the people voted for him.
   B. Native Americans liked Andrew Jackson, and they helped to elect him.
   C. Jackson was elected by the frontier people who had gained the right to vote.
   D. Politicians in Washington wanted Jackson to win, so they voted for him.

2. **How were Native Americans removed from the Southeast?**
   A. The settlers who lived in the Southeast helped the Native Americans find a better place to live.
   B. The Chickasaw and Choctaw went to war with the U.S. Army but lost.
   C. Most Native Americans left their homelands peacefully.
   D. Native Americans were forced by the U.S. Army to march west.

3. **How did the design of mills begin in the United States?**
   A. Germans copied mills they worked in before coming to the U.S.
   B. Samuel Slater brought the design for mills in his head when he came to America.
   C. After Eli Whitney built factories for muskets, he began to build cotton mills.
   D. Robert Fulton bought the plans from a friend in England.

4. **Why were many mills built in New England?**
   A. There were many girls who wanted to work in factories in New England.
   B. Much cotton was grown in New England and was easily transported to the mills.
   C. There were many waterfalls in New England to provide power for the mills.
   D. Expert weavers and spinners lived in New England and wanted to create designs for cloth made in the mills.

5. **The inventor of both the cotton gin and interchangeable parts was—**
   A. Eli Whitney
   B. Solomon Northrup
   C. Nat Turner
   D. Robert Fulton

Name _____ Date _____

6. **How did the economies of the North and the South differ?**

   A. The economy of the North depended on fishing and trading, but in the South the economy focused on service industries.

   B. Northerners made things by hand, but southerners depended on factories.

   C. The North's economy was industrial, and the South's economy was agricultural.

   D. In the North, many people worked in small family-owned businesses, and in the South the economy was built around large businesses.

7. **What effect did the invention of the cotton gin have on slavery?**

   A. The invention of the cotton gin made it possible for machines to pick cotton, so fewer slaves were needed and many were freed.

   B. The invention of the cotton gin made it very profitable to grow cotton, and many slaves were needed in the South where cotton was grown.

   C. After it was invented, many plantation owners sent their families to work in the fields to grow more cotton, so the slaves had more help.

   D. The slaves had to work harder than ever, because the price of cotton fell and the plantation owners couldn't afford to hire more workers.

8. **What was an *abolitionist*?**

   A. someone who fought against slavery

   B. one who was against drinking alcohol

   C. a person who drove a train

   D. the leader of a volunter group

9. **What was the *Underground Railroad*?**

   A. a train that went through tunnels under the ground to free slaves

   B. the name of a book written to tell others about the evils of slavery

   C. a secret network of men and women who led enslaved workers to freedom

   D. the movement to reform the educational system of the United States

10. **Who was Sojourner Truth?**

   A. an African American woman who fought against slavery and for women's rights

   B. a teacher and writer who crusaded to improve the treatment of the mentally ill

   C. an American artist who painted scenes of typical American life in the 1800s

   D. the author of one of the first textbooks, which taught citizenship

Chapter Review

Name _____ Date _____

Vocabulary Strategy: Getting Meaning From Context

# Texas and the Mexican War

When you find unfamiliar words in your reading, **context clues** can help you guess their meanings. These are clues found in nearby words, sentences, or paragraphs.

**1.** **Read these sentences from page 400. Underline clues to the meaning of *bargain*.**

*"The people holding the land grants then sold the land to settlers for the low price of 10¢ an acre. To many . . . this was a bargain, especially since land in the United States was selling for $1.25 an acre."*

Using context clues, you know that *bargain* means "a price that is very good for the buyer."

**2–5.** **Write the context clues you find for each word in the first column. Then underline the correct meaning of each word.**

| Words | Context Clues | Meaning |
|---|---|---|
| **vast**<br>(page 399) | | **A.** *heavily populated*<br>**B.** *very large in area*<br>**C.** *beautiful* |
| **encouraged**<br>(page 400) | | **A.** *prevented something from happening*<br>**B.** *forced people to do something*<br>**C.** *helped make something to happen* |
| **opposed**<br>(page 402) | | **A.** *were in favor of*<br>**B.** *were not in favor of*<br>**C.** *closely examined* |
| **surrendered**<br>(page 403) | | **A.** *agreed to give up*<br>**B.** *refused to give up*<br>**C.** *traded* |

Use each word below in a sentence that shows its meaning.

**6. surrendered** _____

**7. vast** _____

Name _____ Date _____

# Texas and the Mexican War

Review pages 399-403 to answer these questions. Choose the best answer. Circle the letter next to your choice.

1. **What was the Alamo?**
   A. the name of the first Texas army
   B. a river that flowed through Texas
   C. an old mission in San Antonio
   D. a small town in Mexico

2. **Why would the promise of land draw American settlers to Texas?**
   A. Land was valued for farming and ranching.
   B. Cities were becoming overcrowded in the North.
   C. Texas was not involved in the fight over slavery.
   D. The Mexican government was fair.

3. **What does *annexation* mean?**
   A. the joining of a country or other territory to a nation
   B. the holding of land grants which were sold for low prices
   C. the moving of people from one country to another for economic reasons
   D. the establishment of taxes to be paid by citizens of a state

4. **What was the impact of the Mexican War?**
   A. Many Mexicans moved to the East Coast.
   B. Mexico surrendered almost half its territory to the U.S.
   C. Texas gained its independence, but many missed the stable Mexican government and returned to Mexico.
   D. Mexico City became the new capitol of Texas.

5. **What does *dispute* mean?**
   A. to capture
   B. to expand
   C. to argue
   D. to surrender

Lesson Review

Name _____ Date _____

*Environment and Society*

# How Did Countries Agree on Borders?

Nations need clearly defined borders to prevent disagreements.

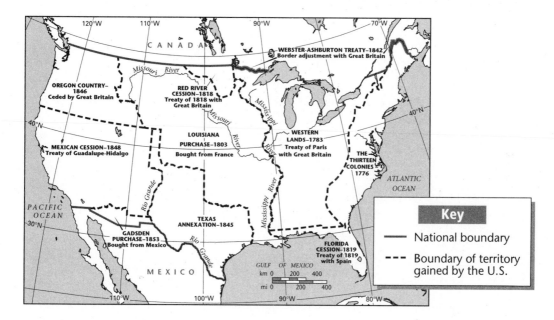

Use the map above to answer the following questions. Write your answers on the map and below.

1. **Color and label the physical feature that determined the western border of the thirteen colonies.**

2. **In the 1840s, many Americans believed the United States should own all of Oregon Country up to latitude 54°-40'N. In which present-day country is that latitude located?** _____

3. **Trace the northern and southern U.S. borders. Which border is larger? How much larger is it? How long would it take an airplane traveling at 200 m.p.h. to patrol each border?** _____

   _____

Think Like a Geographer

Name _____     Date _____

# Borders Within Borders

Use the map above to complete the following questions.

1. **Find your state. Mark physical borders in one color and human-made borders in another. Make a key to show what each color represents.**

2. **Choose another 3 states. Are their borders physical, human-made, or a combination of both? Show them on the map using the colors from your key.**

Name _____ Date _____

Comprehension Skill: Making Decisions

# Across the Continent

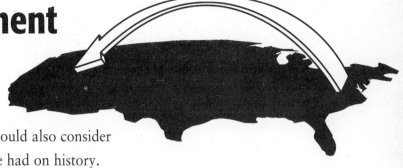

When you read about **decisions** people
have made in the past, you should
consider the **reasons** for their decisions
and the **effects** of those decisions. You should also consider
what effect different decisions might have had on history.

1.  **Reread the section called "The Oregon Trail" on pages 407–408. Then
    answer this question: "What were some of the reasons American settlers
    had for moving west?" Write your answer in the box.**

    ┌─────────────────────────────────────────────────────────────┐
    │ **Reasons for moving west:**                                 │
    │                                                             │
    │                                                             │
    │                                                             │
    │                                                             │
    └─────────────────────────────────────────────────────────────┘

2.  **Read the section called "Other Trails West" on page 409. Then answer
    this question: "What were some of the other reasons settlers had for
    moving west?" Add these to the box above.**

3.  **Why did the Mormons decide to move west?**

    _____

    _____

4.  **How might the West be different today if fewer settlers had decided to
    move there?**

    _____

    _____

Name _____ Date _____

# Across the Continent

Review pages 406-409 to answer these questions. Choose the best answer. Circle the letter next to your choice.

1. **What is a *pass*?**
   A. the highest point on a mountain
   B. an opening through the mountains
   C. a river that cuts through a valley
   D. a land with a mild climate and fertile soil

2. **Who was Jedediah Strong Smith?**
   A. a passenger on the first railroad to travel West
   B. a pioneer who traveled on the Oregon Trail in the late 1800s
   C. a mountain man who roamed the American West in the early 1800s
   D. one of the founders of Salt Lake City

3. **What led American settlers to cross the Great Plains in large numbers during the 1840s?**
   A. the Gold Rush in San Francisco
   B. the opening of the Oregon Trail and the promise of a "pioneer's paradise"
   C. the opportunity to join the military in Fort Vancouver
   D. the invention of the railroad

4. **Who were the first settlers to travel over South Pass?**
   A. railroad engineers taking the first train over the South Pass
   B. farmers who were going to plant apple orchards
   C. missionaries hoping to convert Native Americans to Christianity
   D. travelers from the East who had gone bankrupt and were starting over out West

5. **How did many people travel west to Oregon?**
   A. by train
   B. by covered wagon
   C. by foot
   D. on mules

Lesson Review

Name _____ Date _____

Reading a Contour Map

# Ups and Downs

This contour map shows the elevations of an area near the Oregon Trail in Wyoming.

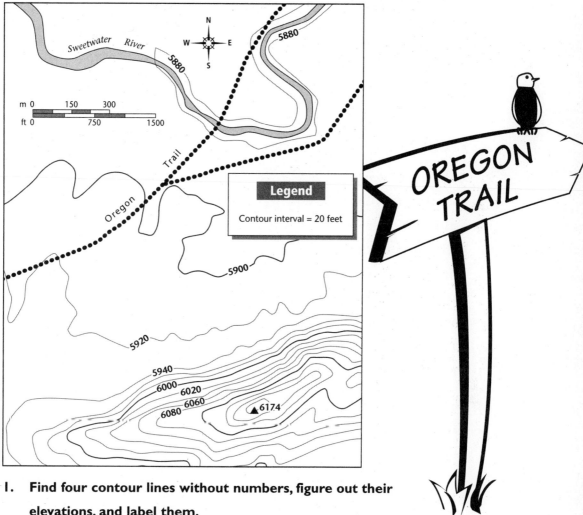

1. **Find four contour lines without numbers, figure out their elevations, and label them.**

2. **Why do you think some of the contour lines are darker than others?**

   _____

3. **What would be the easiest way to hike up to the peak (gentle slopes not steep cliffs)? Mark your path with a dashed line. Explain your reasoning.**

   _____

Name _____ Date _____

Reading a Contour Map

# An Island of Volcanoes

This contour map shows three volcanoes on Hawaii.

1. **Find the southern tip of the island. Count on the contour lines up to the 2500-foot line. Label the 2000-foot contour line.**

2. **Color code the major contour lines. Choose a different color for each box in the legend. Then trace over the corresponding contour lines on the map in colors to match the legend.**

3. **Find Kilauea. Use contour lines to estimate its height.**

_____

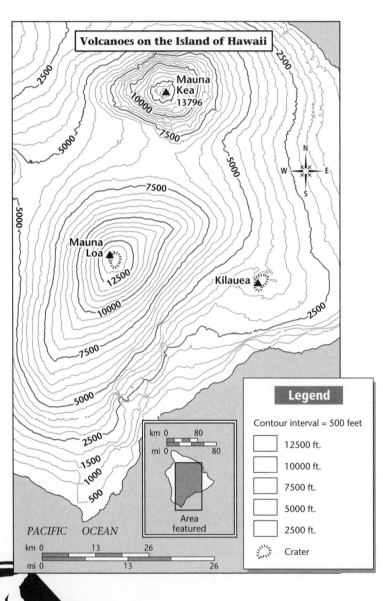

**Volcanoes on the Island of Hawaii**

2500
2500
Mauna Kea ▲ 13796
10000
7500
5000
5000
N
W E
S
7500
Mauna Loa ▲ 12500
Kilauea ▲
10000
2500
7500
5000
2500
1500
1000
500

PACIFIC    OCEAN

km 0        13        26
mi 0            13            26

km 0        80
mi 0            80

Area featured

**Legend**

Contour interval = 500 feet

| | 12500 ft. |
| | 10000 ft. |
| | 7500 ft. |
| | 5000 ft. |
| | 2500 ft. |
| ⟨⟨⟨ | Crater |

Name _____ Date _____

## Comprehension Strategy: Self-Monitoring

# Mining the West

While you are reading, stop from time to time to ask yourself whether you understand the information in your book. You may need to reread some passages or look up some unfamiliar words in the dictionary. This process is called **self-monitoring.**

Read the section called "The California Gold Rush" on pages 414–415, including the Focus question. Look for answers to the Focus question. Answer the question on the lines below.

1. **Focus Question:** What impact did the discovery of gold in California have on that territory?

    _____

    _____

Read the section called "Mining the Mountains" on pages 416–417, including the Focus question. Then answer the Focus question on the lines below.

2. **Focus Question:** What role did mining play in the settlement of the West?

    _____

    _____

3. **Write a short description of the Comstock Lode. If necessary, reread the section of the lesson that tells about this event.**

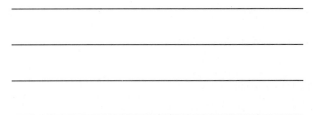

   _____

   _____

   _____

   _____

Name _____ Date _____

# Mining the West

Review pages 414-417 to answer these questions. Choose the best answer. Circle the letter next to your choice.

1.  **What event took place in California in 1849?**
    A.  the Gold Rush
    B.  the opening of blue jeans factories
    C.  the annexation of California
    D.  the Oregon Trail

2.  **Why did California's population increase rapidly in the late 1840s?**
    A.  Land was given to settlers for free.
    B.  People came there to find gold.
    C.  Immigrants moved there to work in factories.
    D.  Promise of a perfect climate attracted new settlers.

3.  **What happened to California's Native American population between 1845 and 1870?**
    A.  It declined because Native Americans moved to Nevada.
    B.  It decreased due to disease and violence.
    C.  It increased, because many of their families came to work in mines.
    D.  It stayed about the same, because they wanted to mine, too.

4.  **Which immigrant group came to California during the Gold Rush?**
    A.  the Bulgarians
    B.  the Ethiopians
    C.  the Chinese
    D.  the Vietnamese

5.  **What was a *boomtown*?**
    A.  a town that grew quickly in population and wealth
    B.  a town where dynamite was used to blast mines
    C.  a town with many factories
    D.  a town with many earthquakes

Lesson Review

Name _____ Date _____

# Moving West

Review pages 398-419 to answer these questions. Choose the best answer. Circle the letter next to your choice.

1. **Which is true about Texas as it became an independent nation?**
   A. The Texans defeated the Mexican army at the Alamo.
   B. As new settlers moved to Texas, they were outnumbered by the French.
   C. As the Texan population grew, they demanded to be part of Louisiana.
   D. The Mexicans tried to stop them, but the Texans defeated the Mexican army under Santa Anna at San Jacinto.

2. **What was the result of the battle at the Alamo?**
   A. The small number of Texas soldiers there defeated Santa Anna's army and declared victory.
   B. Almost all of the Texans there died, but the battle united other Texans in their fight for independence.
   C. Mexico won the battle and Texas retreated until one year later when Texas won its independence.
   D. Santa Anna fought the Texans for 12 days until Sam Houston surrendered.

3. **Who opposed the annexation of Texas and why?**
   A. Mexico—because it didn't want to lose this land to the U.S.
   B. the South—because Texas would compete with them in growing cotton
   C. the North—because it would add another slave state to the U.S.
   D. the West—because they feared new laws would come as a result

4. **What is *Manifest Destiny*?**
   A. a treaty in which Mexico gave almost half of its land to the U.S.
   B. the belief that the U.S. had the right and the duty to expand throughout North America
   C. a bitter dispute between Mexico and the United States over the border and how it should be patrolled
   D. the right for a country to determine its own government and belief system

Name _____ Date _____

5.  **What is the _Continental Divide_?**

    A.  a stretch of high land that separates North America

    B.  a place that marked the halfway point on the Oregon Trail

    C.  the boundary between the United States and the free territories to the west

    D.  the border between the United States and Canada

6.  **The Oregon Trail led from—**

    A.  the Columbia River to the Mississippi River

    B.  Portland, Oregon, to Salt Lake City

    C.  Santa Fe to Oregon

    D.  Independence, Missouri, to Portland, Oregon

7.  **Which trail did Brigham Young and his group follow?**

    A.  the California Trail

    B.  the Trail of Tears

    C.  the Mormon Trail

    D.  the Santa Fe Trail

8.  **Who were more successful than the miners in California?**

    A.  the fur traders

    B.  the merchants

    C.  the Native American traders

    D.  the forty-niners

9.  **What mineral was discovered in Nevada?**

    A.  coal

    B.  silver

    C.  copper

    D.  iron ore

10. **What often happened when the mining in many boomtowns ended?**

    A.  People opened factories there.

    B.  They became centers of trade.

    C.  Fishing and hunting became the main occupations of people there.

    D.  They became ghost towns.

Name _____ Date _____

Comprehension Skill: Understanding Cause and Effect

# Compromises and Conflicts

A **cause** is an event or condition that makes something else happen. An **effect** is an event or condition that results from a cause. A series of causes and effects is a **cause-effect chain**.

**1–2.** **Reread the first paragraph of the section called "Compromises Between North and South" on page 426. Then complete the cause-effect chain below.**

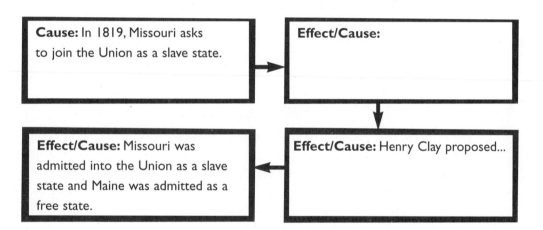

**Cause:** In 1819, Missouri asks to join the Union as a slave state.

**Effect/Cause:**

**Effect/Cause:** Henry Clay proposed...

**Effect/Cause:** Missouri was admitted into the Union as a slave state and Maine was admitted as a free state.

**3–4.** **Read the section called "From Dred Scott to John Brown" on page 428. Then complete the cause-effect chain below.**

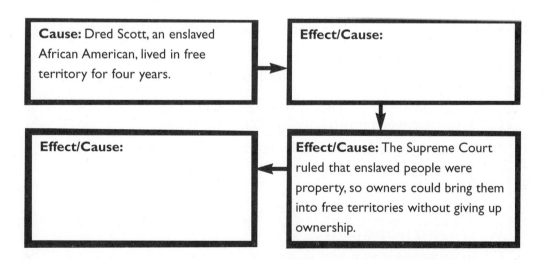

**Cause:** Dred Scott, an enslaved African American, lived in free territory for four years.

**Effect/Cause:**

**Effect/Cause:** The Supreme Court ruled that enslaved people were property, so owners could bring them into free territories without giving up ownership.

**Effect/Cause:**

Name _____  Date _____

# Compromises and Conflicts

Review pages 425-429 to answer these questions. Choose the best answer. Circle the letter next to your choice.

1. **What was a *slave state*?**

   A. a state against slavery

   B. a state that permitted slavery

   C. a state where slaves could go to hide

   D. a state which was waiting to become part of the U.S.

2. **What was the *Union*?**

   A. another name for the American flag

   B. the states that allowed slavery

   C. the states joined together under the Constitution

   D. the railroad that carried the first settlers across the U.S.

3. **What was the purpose of the Missouri Compromise?**

   A. to require by law that people capture escaped slaves and return them to slavery

   B. to agree that the North and South would not go to war

   C. to make the number of slave and free states equal

   D. to guarantee more slave states in the South to help plantation owners

4. **Why did compromises fail to stop the conflict between the North and the South?**

   A. There were more states in the North than in the South.

   B. As more compromises were made, more antislavery books were written.

   C. A war had begun between the North and the South.

   D. New actions, such as the Dred Scott case, eliminated the compromises.

5. **What does *secede* mean?**

   A. to withdraw or break away from

   B. to capture escaped slaves

   C. to strengthen laws against slavery

   D. to vote for compromise

Lesson Review

Name _____ Date _____

*Places and Regions*

# How Did Regions Vote in 1860?

In the presidential elections of 1860, regional loyalty was more important to voters than loyalty to a particular political party. This map shows states and regions of the United States in 1860.

Use the map and the information in the chart to answer the questions below. Write your answers on the map and on the lines below.

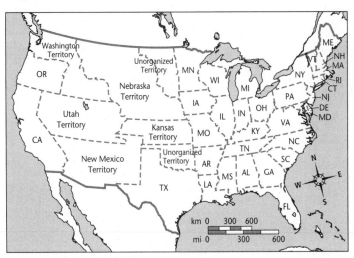

| Results of 1860 Presidential Election | |
|---|---|
| **Candidate/Party** | **States Won** |
| John Bell/Constitutional Union/TN | KY, TN, VA |
| John Breckinridge/Democratic/KY | Al, AR, DE, FL, GA, LA, MD, MS, NC, SC, TX |
| Stephen Douglas/Democratic/IL | MO, 1/2 of NJ (north) |
| Abraham Lincoln/Republican/IL | CA, CT, IL, IN, IA, ME, MD, MA, MI, MN, NH, 1/2 of NJ (south), NY, OH, OR, PA, RI, VT, WI |

**You'll need:** 4 colored markers or pencils

1. **Color in the states that each candidate won in the 1860 election. Use a different color to represent each candidate. Make a color key.**

2. **Which candidates won their home states?**

   _____

3. **What do the election results in Oregon and California tell you about how voters in these states felt about slavery?**

   _____

   _____

Think Like a Geographer

Workbook for Reading and Review    **171**

Name _____   Date _____

# The Compromises

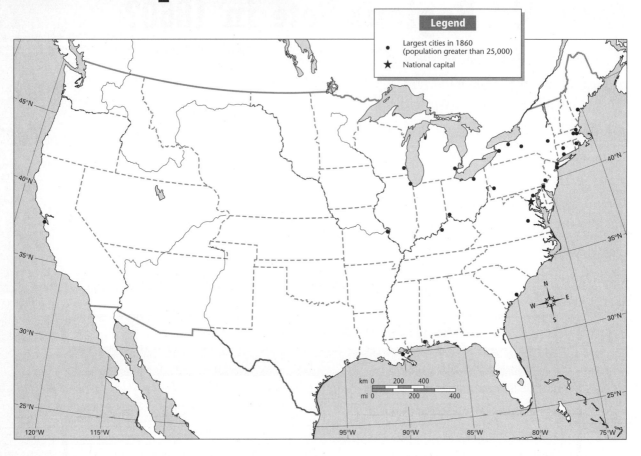

Use the map above to answer the following questions.

1.  **Using your text as a guide, outline the free and slave states of 1854 in two colors.**

2.  **Color the states of the Union and the Confederacy in two different colors.**

3.  **What pattern do you see? Which states don't follow this pattern? Why do you think this is so?**

_____

_____

_____

Name _____  Date _____

Vocabulary Skill: Key Vocabulary

# Marching to Battle

The first page of Lesson 2 lists five **Key Vocabulary** words and phrases: *civil war, mobilize, volunteer, blockade,* and *siege*. Knowing these words will help you understand this lesson.

Draw a line to match each word or phrase with its meaning. If you need help, try rereading the part of Lesson 2 where the term first appears.

**1. volunteer** (page 433)

**A.** a war fought between regions of one nation

**2. mobilize** (page 433)

**B.** stop traffic from entering or leaving an area so goods cannot be shipped out or supplies brought in

**3. lay siege to** (page 436)

**C.** surround a city or area and keep out food and other supplies until its inhabitants give up

**4. civil war** (page 432)

**D.** a person who chooses to become a soldier

**5. blockade** (page 435)

**E.** prepare for

Answer the questions below with complete sentences.

**6.** *Blockading* **a harbor might be one part of** *laying siege* **to a city. Explain why.**

_____

_____

**7. How is a** *civil war* **different from other types of war you've read about?**

_____

_____

Reading and Vocabulary Strategies

Name _____     Date _____

# Marching to Battle

Review pages 432-437 to answer these questions. Choose the best answer. Circle the letter next to your choice.

1. **What is a *civil war*?**

   A. a war fought between two countries

   B. a war fought between regions of one nation

   C. a war fought on horseback

   D. a war with many casualties

2. **Which of the following advantages belonged to the South?**

   A. the best generals in the country

   B. larger population

   C. more industry

   D. money

3. **What does *mobilize* mean?**

   A. to defend one's home

   B. to move secretly through the countryside

   C. to prepare for war

   D. to become a soldier

4. **What was the importance of the First Battle of Bull Run?**

   A. It proved that the North could protect its ports.

   B. It showed the North that the South would not easily be defeated.

   C. It was the last battle of the war.

   D. The North won with an army of common men and no trained leaders.

5. **What does *blockade* mean?**

   A. to send goods on a ship

   B. to build a ship that cannot be destroyed

   C. to flee to another city in a panic

   D. to stop all traffic entering or leaving ports

Name _____ Date _____

Comparing Historical Images

# Two Views of History

Although photography had been invented before the Civil War, the war images most people saw were drawings published in newspapers. Look at the photograph of the Confederate fort on page 439 of your textbook. Think about how people would have reacted to a drawing of this same scene.

Answer the questions below.

1. **What did you think when you first saw the photograph of the Confederate fort?**

   _____

   _____

2. **If you saw a drawing of the Confederate fort instead of a photograph, would you have reacted differently? Why?**

   _____

   _____

3. **Based on the photograph, how do you think the fort was built? Why do you think so much of it is underground?**

   _____

   _____

4. **Write your own caption for the photograph.**

   _____

   _____

Name _____  Date _____

Comparing Historical Images

# Two Drummer Boys

Compare the painting of a Civil War drummer boy on page 442 to the photograph of another Civil War drummer boy on page 445.

1.  **What similarities do you see between the two boys?  What differences?**

    _____

    _____

    _____

    _____

2.  **Do you think the painter and photographer had the same opinion about military service?  Explain.  How was the boy in each image posed and portrayed to get across the artist's point of view?**

    _____

    _____

    _____

    _____

3.  **How does seeing both images help you better understand the life of a Civil War drummer boy?**

    _____

    _____

    _____

    _____

Name _____ Date _____

Comprehension Skill: Topic, Main Idea, and Supporting Details

# African Americans Join the Fight

The **topic** of a passage is the subject that the sentences tell about. The **main idea** sums up what the author says about the topic. **Supporting details** give more information about the main idea.

**1–2.** Reread the paragraph on pages 445–446 that begins, "Around the same time . . . ." Add two supporting details to the chart below.

**Topic:** Ending slavery

**Main Idea:** For several reasons, Lincoln began to think about ending slavery.

**Supporting Detail:** Enslaved African Americans were being forced to help the South.

**Supporting Detail:**

**Supporting Detail:**

**Supporting Detail:** Many northerners believed in freeing enslaved African Americans.

**3–5.** Reread the section called "Among the Bravest of Soldiers" on page 447. Add three supporting details to the chart below.

**Topic:** African Americans who fought for the Union

**Main Idea:** African American soldiers greatly helped the Union war effort.

**Supporting Detail:**

**Supporting Detail:**

**Supporting Detail:**

Name _____ Date _____

# African Americans Join the Fight

Review pages 444-447 to answer these questions. Choose the best answer. Circle the letter next to your choice.

1. **Why did many African Americans believe the Union was fighting the South?**
   A. to gain freedom from the South
   B. to preserve the unity of America
   C. to take over their land and make the North larger
   D. to end slavery

2. **Why was President Lincoln fighting the Civil War?**
   A. because he opposed slavery
   B. to save the Union
   C. to increase the size of the United States
   D. to end border disputes with Canada and Mexico

3. **What was the Emancipation Proclamation?**
   A. a law giving rights to African Americans
   B. part of the Underground Railroad
   C. a campaign to enlist African Americans as soldiers
   D. a document stating that all enslaved people in the Confederate states would be free

4. **What is *contraband*?**
   A. massive gunfire
   B. property taken from the enemy
   C. a regiment made up of African American soldiers
   D. a letter to the President

5. **Why was Lincoln hesitant to enlist African American soldiers?**
   A. He was afraid that Missouri, Kentucky, Maryland, and Delaware would secede.
   B. He thought they might not be loyal to the North.
   C. He was afraid they might file freedom suits against him.
   D. He didn't have money to feed additional troops.

Name _____ Date _____

Comprehension Strategy: K-W-L

# Behind the Lines of Battle

In Lesson 4, you will read about life for civilians, or people who were not soldiers, during the Civil War. You can use the **K-W-L reading strategy** to help you read this lesson. Here are the steps:

**K:** **Write what you Know.** What do you already know about civilian life during the Civil War? Write this information in the first column of the chart.

**W:** **Write what you Want to learn.** Write questions you have about civilian life during the Civil War in the middle column of the chart.

**L:** **Write what you Learned.** After reading, write what you learned about civilian life during the Civil War in the third column of the chart.

1. **Follow the steps of the K-W-L strategy as you read Lesson 4. Use the chart below.**

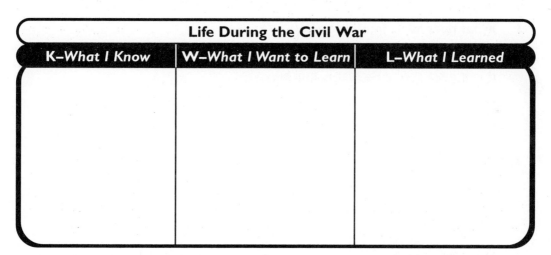

| Life During the Civil War | | |
|---|---|---|
| **K–What I Know** | **W–What I Want to Learn** | **L–What I Learned** |
|  |  |  |

2. **After reading, cross out any items in the "K" column that you have learned are not correct. Write the correct facts in the "L" column.**

3. **Put a check beside each question in the "W" column that was answered by the lesson. Write those answers in the "L" column. Write an X beside each question that was not answered and think of where you might find the answer.**

Name _____     Date _____

# Behind the Lines of Battle

Review pages 448-451 to answer these questions. Choose the best answer. Circle the letter next to your choice.

1. **How did harvest time change during the war?**
   A.  Less crops were grown and harvested since many farmers went to war.
   B.  Women were now in the fields harvesting the crops.
   C.  There was no harvest time during the war because machine parts were needed to make guns.
   D.  Harvesting was done when the men were home.

2. **Who was Clara Barton?**
   A.  one of the first women doctors
   B.  a spy for the Confederate army
   C.  the inventor of a faster harvesting machine
   D.  the founder of the American Red Cross

3. **What does *home front* describe?**
   A.  the front doors of homes that were decorated with flags and patriotic symbols
   B.  the place where a war is fought
   C.  a secret hiding place on a farm where military spies could hide
   D.  people who are not in the military, but live in a country that is at war

4. **What is a *civilian*?**
   A.  a person who pays taxes
   B.  someone who fights in a war
   C.  a person who is not in the military
   D.  someone who takes care of wounded people

5. **What is the *draft*?**
   A.  the giving away of food to feed soldiers
   B.  a system of choosing people and forcing them to join the army
   C.  a note that states the cost of an item
   D.  an order by the government to pay taxes on crops

Name _____  Date _____

# A House Divided

Review pages 424-453 to answer these questions. Choose the best answer. Circle the letter next to your choice.

1. **How did new territory cause conflicts over slavery?**
   A. New territories admitted as states could upset the balance between slave and free states.
   B. Settlers in the American West often led protests against slavery, which upset Americans in the rest of the country.
   C. Many settlers in the American West wanted to have enslaved people help them build new homes and start farms, but the South wouldn't allow it.
   D. Slaves often ran away to the frontier and new territories, so the people who lived there voted against slavery.

2. **What did the Kansas-Nebraska Act state?**
   A. that settlers in Kansas and Nebraska could own slaves if they chose to do so
   B. that settlers could vote to determine whether they would be slave or free
   C. that Americans had the right to publish abolitionist newspapers
   D. that enslaved people had the right to go to court and live in free territory

3. **What does *confederate* mean?**
   A. another name for a compromise
   B. part of a group united for a common purpose
   C. one who is against slavery
   D. a candidate who runs against the President

4. **How did the Union begin to gain the advantage in 1863?**
   A. The Union won the Battle of Bull Run.
   B. The Confederate army lost many men to diseases and starvation.
   C. The Confederates retreated after losing one of their best generals on the *Monitor*.
   D. The Union won the battles of Vicksburg and Gettysburg.

Name _____  Date _____

5. **Why did Lincoln finally allow African Americans to join the Union army?**

   A.  because African Americans wrote a petition

   B.  because the Union needed soldiers

   C.  because they threatened to move south again

   D.  because African Americans showed him they could ride horses

6. **What does *emancipation* mean?**

   A.  slavery

   B.  fighting

   C.  freedom

   D.  winning

7. **How did African Americans help the Union war effort?**

   A.  by freeing slaves in the South

   B.  by fighting as soldiers

   C.  by becoming politicians

   D.  by building southern factories

8. **What hardships faced people on the home front?**

   A.  It was hard to get flags during the war because there was less money.

   B.  Children didn't get a good education because teachers were off fighting.

   C.  Hardships included food shortages, hunger, inflation, and unfair draft laws.

   D.  Even rich people were chosen by the government to go to war.

9. **What is *inflation*?**

   A.  the wages earned by a working person in one year

   B.  a sacrifice made by citizens to help soldiers keep fighting

   C.  a drop in the value of money and a rise in prices

   D.  a shortage of food despite plenty of crops being grown

10. **Why were some northerners angered by the draft?**

   A.  Poor people who competed with African Americans for jobs were angry, because they didn't want to fight a war to end slavery.

   B.  Some northerners wanted to move but were afraid of paying higher taxes.

   C.  Northerners resented having to share their food with the soldiers.

   D.  Northerners didn't like the government fixing costs on their goods.

Name _____ Date _____

Comprehension Strategy: Adjust Reading Rate

# A Union Preserved

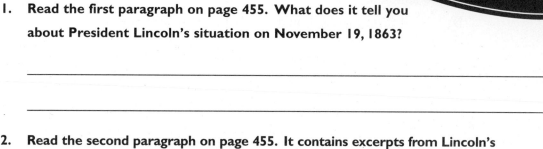

Your textbook includes *quotations* (things people said or wrote) and *excerpts* (parts) from historical documents. When these are difficult, slow your **reading rate** to better understand the passage.

Answer the questions below with complete sentences.

1. **Read the first paragraph on page 455. What does it tell you about President Lincoln's situation on November 19, 1863?**

   _____

   _____

2. **Read the second paragraph on page 455. It contains excerpts from Lincoln's Gettysburg Address. What is one idea Lincoln talked about in this speech?**

   _____

3. **Now slowly reread the second paragraph on page 455. What did President Lincoln say in his speech about the birth of the United States? Answer in your own words.**

   _____

   _____

4. **In President Lincoln's opinion, what was the important task that faced survivors of the Civil War? Answer in your own words.**

   _____

   _____

5. **Why do you think President Lincoln said what he did in his speech?**

   _____

   _____

Name _____  Date _____

# A Union Preserved

Review pages 455-459 to answer these questions. Choose the best answer. Circle the letter next to your choice.

1. **Why did Lincoln speak to the people at Gettysburg?**
   A. to tell them that the Civil War was over
   B. to tell them that their sacrifices were not in vain
   C. to announce that he would run for reelection
   D. to tell them that he would resign if they lost the war

2. **Why were Grant's strategies against the South successful?**
   A. He cut off the Confederate army from food and supplies.
   B. He knew how to fight in the southern back country.
   C. Grant had once been a southerner and knew how the South would fight the war.
   D. Grant had many spies in the South who gave him valuable information.

3. **What does *desertion* mean?**
   A. for an army to fight a battle in the desert
   B. for a soldier to run away from the army
   C. for two groups in a country to fight against each other
   D. for people to be against slavery

4. **The murder of a president or other political figure is called—**
   A. election
   B. confederation
   C. assassination
   D. discrimination

5. **Why was the surrender of Robert E. Lee one of the most important events of American history?**
   A. It showed the world that the South disapproved of slavery.
   B. Never before had an American general surrendered during a battle.
   C. It tripled the size of the United States as new lands were gained.
   D. It made the United States one country again.

Lesson Review

Name _____ Date _____

Comprehension Strategy: Summarizing a Lesson

# Freedom's Challenge

**Summarizing** means retelling important ideas in your own words. Follow the steps below to summarize Lesson 2.

**Step 1:** After you have read the lesson once, scan the text again. Write the topic of Lesson 2 in the box below.

**Topic:**

**Step 2:** Reread any parts of the lesson that confused you.

**Step 3:** Write the main ideas from each section of the lesson in the boxes below. Include ideas from visuals, captions, and special features.

**Main ideas from "The Promise of Freedom,"** pages 462-463

**Main ideas from "Black Codes and Sharecropping,"** pages 463-465

**Step 4:** Use the information you wrote above to write a summary of the lesson on another sheet of paper.

Name _____ Date _____

# Freedom's Challenge

Review pages 462-465 to answer these questions. Choose the best answer. Circle the letter next to your choice.

1. **What were the hopes of many newly freed African Americans?**
   A. for a free place to live in another country
   B. for a chance to work for someone else for pay
   C. for full freedom and land of their own
   D. for their former owners to pay them for all the work they had done

2. **What does *redistribute* mean?**
   A. to decide who has power again
   B. to divide and sell property
   C. to farm the land again
   D. to help former enslaved persons

3. **Who were *freedmen*?**
   A. people who gave free homes and food to newly freed African Americans
   B. African Americans who had been enslaved before the Civil War
   C. members of churches who shared their homes with former enslaved people
   D. government officials who helped African Americans travel to other countries

4. **What is *credit*?**
   A. doing something to earn extra money
   B. buying something without paying for it right away
   C. telling someone the cost of an item
   D. putting money in a bank

5. **How did many African Americans feel after the war was over?**
   A. disappointed because they couldn't make enough money
   B. joyful that they could no longer be bought or sold
   C. frustrated because they were still dependent on others
   D. all of the above

Lesson Review

Name _____ Date _____

Comprehension Skill: Categorizing

# Rebuilding the South

You have learned that one way to help you understand and remember what you read is to organize facts into **categories,** or groups.

1-2. **Read the introduction on page 468 and the section called "Radical Republicans." Write facts about these two groups in the chart below to help you understand how each wanted Reconstruction to work.**

| Radical Republicans and Reconstruction | Democrats and Reconstruction |
|---|---|
| | |

3-5. **Reread the section called "Reconstruction" on pages 470–472. It describes three groups of people who led the South after the Civil War. Write the name of each group above a column in the chart. Then add facts and details about each group to the chart.**

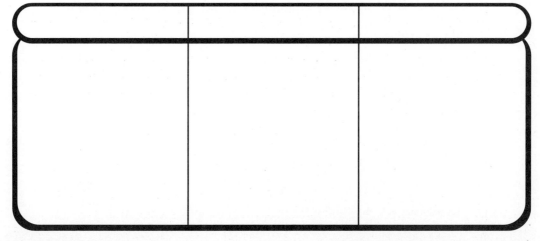

Name _____ Date _____

# Rebuilding the South

Review pages 468-472 to answer these questions. Choose the best answer. Circle the letter next to your choice.

1.  **Who became the President after Lincoln?**
    A.  Andrew Johnson
    B.  Thaddeus Stevens
    C.  Rutherford B. Hayes
    D.  General Grant

2.  **What war broke out after the Civil War?**
    A.  World War I
    B.  the Canadian War
    C.  the War Against the Black Codes
    D.  a political war between people who didn't agree about rebuilding the South

3.  **What was *Reconstruction*?**
    A.  taking away the rights of African Americans again
    B.  building the South again after the Civil War
    C.  giving all citizens the right to vote again
    D.  forbidding any state from denying rights to U.S. citizens

4.  **Which of the following ideas was part of Andrew Johnson's plan for Reconstruction?**
    A.  African Americans should move to the North.
    B.  The federal government should decide how the states should govern their citizens.
    C.  The southern states should be allowed to pass Black Codes.
    D.  all of the above

5.  **What does *impeach* mean?**
    A.  to help African Americans
    B.  to accuse the President of being unfit
    C.  to move to the North from the South
    D.  to harvest peaches and exchange them for plantation land

Lesson Review

Name _____ Date _____

Making Database Searches

# Ask Your Computer

Follow these steps to practice doing a CD-ROM encyclopedia search on a topic related to the Reconsturction period.

1. **First think of a question that will help you focus your research. For example, "What was the Freedmen's Bureau?" What is the key word or phrase in this focus question?** _____

2. **The next step is to begin your search. Most CD-ROM encyclopedias have a *Search* or *Find* button. A box will appear asking for the topic of your search. Write your topic in this sample box below.**

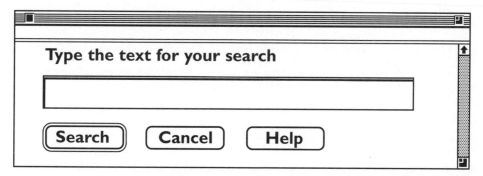

3. **The box below shows search results for "Freedmen's Bureau." Answer the following questions on another sheet of paper.**

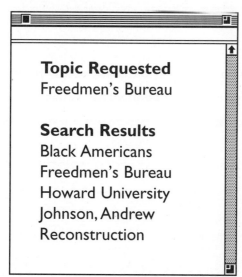

A. You will want to look at subjects that you think will provide the most information about your topic. Which subject would you choose to look at first? Why?

B. Why would it be worthwhile to look at other related subjects?

C. You can print out copies of useful information to refer to later. If the name of the article and the name of the database or encyclopedia does not appear, why should you write this information on the printout?

Name _____  Date _____

Making Database Searches

# Do Your Own Search

Follow these steps to practice searching on a CD-ROM encyclopedia or computer database.

1. **Choose a topic from United States history that you have learned about and that interests you—from the time of early peoples to the Reconstruction. Write a question to focus your research.**

   _____

   _____

2. **Circle the key word or phrase in your question.**

3. **Using your textbook as a guide, list four words that you may find in a CD-ROM encyclopedia or the computer database when using that phrase or word.**

   _____

4. **Are there any other subjects related to your research topic? If so, list them.**

   _____

   _____

5. **What are the advantages of using a computer database or CD-ROM encyclopedia rather than an encyclopedia in book form? What are the disadvantages? Which would you rather use? Write your answers below.**

   _____

   _____

   _____

Name _____ Date _____

# The Nation Reunited

Review pages 454-475 to answer these questions. Choose the best answer. Circle the letter next to your choice.

1. **Whom did northerners blame when the Civil War did not end quickly?**

   A. slaves in the South

   B. Ulysses S. Grant

   C. Abraham Lincoln

   D. the Union soldiers

2. **What did Sherman mean by _total war_?**

   A. a kind of war in which the soldiers kill everyone on the opposing side

   B. a strategy in which everything soldiers can use is destroyed by the enemy

   C. a strategy in which each side's best soldiers fight one final battle

   D. a kind of war in which everyone who wants to is allowed to fight

3. **Where did the surrender take place?**

   A. New York City

   B. Springfield, Illinois

   C. Appomattox Courthouse

   D. Washington, D.C.

4. **What was the meaning of "40 acres and a mule"?**

   A. the knowledge that it takes a lot of land and farm animals to make a profit

   B. the hope that each enslaved person would be given land from former plantations

   C. a dream that every enslaved person could trade a mule for 40 acres of land

   D. a symbol of the small towns founded by former enslaved persons

5. **What laws took away the rights of African Americans?**

   A. The Freedmen's Bureau passed laws to keep African Americans poor.

   B. Congress passed laws that allowed plantation owners to take away land from African Americans.

   C. Black Codes prevented freed people from voting, traveling, or holding certain jobs.

   D. Congress wrote laws that prohibited African Americans from buying land.

Name _____ Date _____

6. **What practices took away the rights of African Americans?**

   A. Credit cards made African Americans rely on others for money.

   B. African Americans were forced to move to the North, away from their homes.

   C. Sharecropping tended to make farmers dependent on landowners.

   D. Growing and selling cotton kept African Americans from getting the education they needed.

7. **What was a problem with sharecropping?**

   A. Many sharecroppers stole money, crops, and farm equipment from the landowners.

   B. The sharecroppers wanted more and more of the landowner's farm and sometimes became violent.

   C. Farmers often had to borrow money after selling their harvests and fell deeper into debt each year.

   D. all of the above

8. **Who were the *Radical Republicans*?**

   A. members of a group that wanted to build a new U.S. capital in the South

   B. a group that worked to pass the Black Codes in the North and the South

   C. Congressmen who tried to help African Americans

   D. a new political party that wanted to elect an African American for President

9. **What impact did Reconstruction have on the South?**

   A. New groups gained more power in southern politics.

   B. Many northerners decided to move there and live on plantations.

   C. The South became more powerful than the North politically.

   D. New cities were built and northern industries moved to the South.

10. **What was a *scalawag*?**

   A. one who moved from the North to the South to start a new business

   B. a white southerner loyal to the Union

   C. a northerner who ran a hotel for visiting southerners

   D. another name for a sharecropper

Chapter Review

Name _____ Date _____

Comprehension Skill: Drawing Conclusions

# Linking the East and West

Sometimes when you read, you have to figure things out that the writer doesn't tell you. This is called **drawing conclusions.** To draw conclusions about topics in your textbook, you can put facts from the text together with information you already know.

Reread page 481. The chart below shows the process of drawing a conclusion based on information from this page.

PONY EXPRESS

| **Facts from the text** | | **Your own knowledge** | | **Conclusion** |
|---|---|---|---|---|
| *The pony express was an important link between western pioneers and the world back East.* | **+** | *In the early 1800s there were no telephones or trains connecting the East and the West.* | **=** | *Before the pony express, people who lived far apart couldn't get important messages to one another easily.* |

1-3.   Now, reread page 482.  Draw a conclusion to answer this question: "How do you explain the fact that the pony express stopped operating in October 1861, the same month and year that telegraph wires reached California?"

| **Facts from the text** | | **Your own knowledge** | | **Conclusion** |
|---|---|---|---|---|
| | **+** | | **=** | |

Reading and Vocabulary Strategies

Name _____  Date _____

# Linking the East and West

Review pages 481-483 to answer these questions. Choose the best answer. Circle the letter next to your choice.

1.  **What was the *pony express*?**
    A.  a ranch in the West where the fastest ponies were raised for racing
    B.  a method of transportation that moved people quickly to the West
    C.  a mail service that kept people across the United States in touch with each other
    D.  the fastest train ever to travel from the East to the West in the 1800s

2.  **Who invented the telegraph?**
    A.  Benjamin Franklin
    B.  Eli Whitney
    C.  Alexander Graham Bell
    D.  Samuel Morse

3.  **How did the telegraph help Americans to communicate?**
    A.  With the telegraph, coast-to-coast communications took only a few minutes.
    B.  This new kind of writing instrument soon replaced paper and ink.
    C.  It saved Americans time because they didn't have to recopy messages.
    D.  People could now speak into a machine and have someone far away hear them.

4.  **What was a *transcontinental railroad*?**
    A.  a train designed to travel very long distances without stopping
    B.  a railroad built by a state and running within that state's borders
    C.  a type of train that was very fast and lightweight
    D.  a railroad that ran across the continent

5.  **What happened at Promontory Point?**
    A.  Congress forced railroad workers to meet there to finish laying rails.
    B.  The first telegraph message was received there.
    C.  It's where the first pony express race was held.
    D.  The first cattle drive began there.

Name _____ Date _____

## Comprehension Skill: Noting Details
# Life on the Plains

Paying attention to **details** in your textbook
can help you gain a better understanding of what you are reading.

1. Read the section called "Plains Indians" on pages 486-489. Write a brief answer to the Focus question: "How did Native Americans respond to the government's reservation policy?"

_____

_____

2-5. To answer to this question more fully, find details about the effects of American westward expansion on Native Americans. Complete the chart below. Remember to look for information in illustrations, captions, and maps, too.

| Questions | Answers |
|---|---|
| Why were buffalo important to Native Americans living on the plains? | |
| How did most settlers feel about the Native Americans who lived on the plains? | |
| What were some of the reasons settlers had for hunting buffalo? | |
| Where did the government force Native Americans to move? | |

Reading and Vocabulary Strategies

Name _____ Date _____

# Life on the Plains

Review pages 484-489 to answer these questions. Choose the best answer. Circle the letter next to your choice.

1. **Who was Nat Love?**
   A. a cowboy born in Tennessee who published his life story in 1907
   B. the owner of the Union Pacific Railroad
   C. a ranch owner in Tennessee
   D. an outlaw and horse thief who was hanged in 1907

2. **How did the cattle industry develop?**
   A. Cattle started migrating across the Mexican border.
   B. Cowboys began writing about their exciting adventures.
   C. More people began eating meat.
   D. Cattle were moved across the plains to northern railroads and shipped east.

3. **What was a *cattle trail*?**
   A. tracks left in prairie grass by covered wagons heading westward
   B. a route across the plains to towns where cattle were shipped to the East
   C. a railroad that transported cattle to the West
   D. a road that had a barbed wire fence along both sides

4. **How did Native Americans respond to the government's reservation policy?**
   A. Some Native Americans agreed to move, but many fought to hold on to their land.
   B. Many Native Americans agreed to move to reservations.
   C. Many Native Americans wore buffalo coats to show their resistance.
   D. none of the above

5. **Why did settlers kill buffalo on the Great Plains?**
   A. They used the meat to feed railroad workers.
   B. They wanted to sell the hides.
   C. They hoped to weaken Native Americans by killing the buffalo.
   D. all of the above

Lesson Review

Name _____ Date _____

## Vocabulary Strategy: Getting Meaning From Context

# Settlers on the Plains

**Context clues** are clues to a word's meaning found in surrounding words and sentences. Context clues are especially helpful for figuring out the meanings of words with more than one definition.

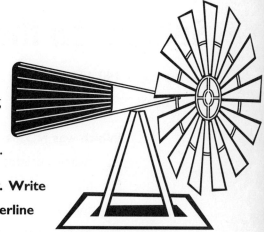

**1-5.** In Lesson 3, find the words in the left column below. Write the context clues you find for each word. Then underline the correct meaning for each word.

| Words | Context Clues | Meanings |
|---|---|---|
| **belongings** (page 491) | | **A.** *things that are owned* **B.** *families* **C.** *unwanted items* |
| **seal** (page 492) | | **A.** *a large sea mammal* **B.** *a device that is used to stamp a design on wax* **C.** *to make secure against leakage* |
| **awe** (page 490) | | **A.** *tiredness* **B.** *amazement* **C.** *anger* |
| **store** (page 492) | | **A.** *a business where people buy things* **B.** *things that are saved for future use* **C.** *to keep for use in the future* |
| **swarms** (page 491) | | **A.** *humming sounds* **B.** *large numbers of insects* **C.** *problems caused by insects* |

Name _____ Date _____

# Settlers on the Plains

Review pages 490-493 to answer these questions. Choose the best answer. Circle the letter next to your choice.

1. **Which was NOT a problem for farmers on the plains?**
   A.  swarms of grasshoppers
   B.  high cost of land
   C.  cold winters
   D.  prairie fires

2. **What is a *homestead*?**
   A.  a settler's log cabin
   B.  a temporary home used by settlers until a house could be built
   C.  a law passed by Congress
   D.  land claimed by a settler

3. **What was a *sodbuster*?**
   A.  a northerner who moved west
   B.  a farmer who only planted grain
   C.  a settler who had to break through thick sod to prepare the land
   D.  a grasshopper that invaded the prairies

4. **What were homes often built of on the prairies?**
   A.  logs
   B.  blocks of sod
   C.  stone
   D.  bundles of dried grass

5. **What was the *Grange*?**
   A.  an organization of farmers
   B.  another name for the Great Plains
   C.  the leader of the farmers in the plains
   D.  a town where farm supplies were sold

Name _____ Date _____

Comparing Maps and Graphs

# A Quilt of Many Peoples

Read and compare this map and graph to learn more about immigration to the
Dakota Territory. Answer the questions below.

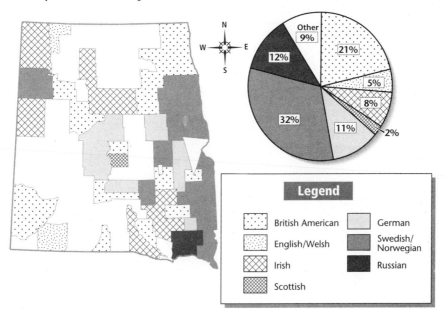

1. **Which was the largest immigrant group to settle in the Dakota Territory? What
   percentage of immigrants were from that group? Where did most of them settle?**

   _____

2. **Find the percentages that show German and Russian immigration. How do they
   compare? Now compare the size of the areas where they settled. How were their
   settlement patterns different?**

   _____

   _____

3. **By looking at just the map, can you tell which were the largest immigrant groups?
   Explain why or why not.**

   _____

   _____

Name _____  Date _____

## Comparing Maps and Graphs

# Alaska's Lands

Study this map and graph to learn who owns Alaska's lands, then answer the questions.

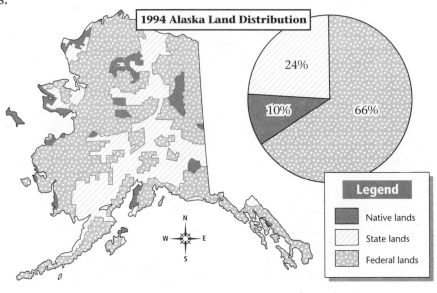

**1994 Alaska Land Distribution**

24%

10%

66%

**Legend**

Native lands

State lands

Federal lands

1. **Who owns most of Alaska's lands? How do you know?**

   _____

2. **Which do you think gives you more information — the graph or the map? Why is it helpful to have both?**

   _____

   _____

3. **One of Alaska's nicknames is "The Last Frontier." What information in the graph and map supports the idea that much of Alaska is unsettled land?**

   _____

   _____

Skills Workshop

Name _____ Date _____

# Reshaping the West

Review pages 480-497 to answer these questions. Choose the best answer. Circle the letter next to your choice.

1. **How long did the pony express last?**

   A. two decades

   B. April 1860 to October 1861

   C. October 1880 to June 1900

   D. three years

2. **What is a *telegraph*?**

   A. a very early form of computer

   B. a way of writing down a message and making several copies of it

   C. a device that uses electrical energy to send signals over wires

   D. a machine that people talk into to send messages to others

3. **How did the transcontinental railroad link East and West?**

   A. People from China could now travel to the western United States.

   B. It made it possible to move raw materials quickly from the West to factories and markets in the East.

   C. Steel could easily be mined and manufactured in the West and then be shipped to Asia.

   D. all of the above

4. **Who did the Central Pacific hire and where did they build?**

   A. They hired mainly Chinese immigrants to lay track to the east starting from Sacramento, California.

   B. They hired only people born in the United States to lay track across the Rocky Mountains.

   C. They hired mostly teenagers to lay track to the south from Canada to Mexico.

   D. They hired mainly German workers to lay track to the west from Philadelphia.

Name _____     Date _____

5.  **What is a _reservation_?**

    A.  not wanting to change to modern methods

    B.  land set aside for Native Americans

    C.  a part of a city where Native Americans lived

    D.  a safe place for buffalo to graze

6.  **Who was Geronimo?**

    A.  the brother of Crazy Horse who led the attack at Little Bighorn

    B.  a Sioux who taught others the Dance of the Ghosts

    C.  an Apache leader who held out the longest against the government

    D.  the son of Sitting Bull who shot General Custer

7.  **What was the Ghost Dance?**

    A.  a dance held the night before a battle to frighten the enemy away

    B.  a custom in which dancers wore white and prayed for their relatives

    C.  a ritual that was believed to bring dead Native American warriors back to life

    D.  Geronimo's vision that showed him the ghosts of dead buffaloes and led him to new hunting grounds

8.  **_Dry farming_ was a technique in which—**

    A.  fields were planted every other season, so the soil could store moisture for the next planting season

    B.  the land was allowed to dry out completely to get rid of diseases in the soil

    C.  seeds were spread evenly on the dry ground and then covered with sod

    D.  only seeds that needed little water were planted because of the shortage of water

9.  **How did the Grange help farmers?**

    A.  by being so large that the land never got worn out

    B.  by going to Washington to fight for farmers' rights

    C.  by letting farmers band together to save money

    D.  by providing a place where farmers could live while building their farms

10. **How did populism help farmers?**

    A.  It gave farmers attention and a strong voice in national politics.

    B.  It helped farmers find the best place to live and work.

    C.  It reminded farmers to be thankful for good harvests.

    D.  It spread new farming tools through newspaper articles and letters.

Name _____   Date _____

Vocabulary Skill: Technical Terms

# Inventions Shape Industry

**Technical terms** are special words and phrases used to discuss a certain topic, like *blast furnace* and *converter*. These words are used to discuss steel production.

Read the introduction to Lesson 1 on page 499, and the paragraph under the heading "Electricity Lights Up America" on page 501. Then read the words in the box below.

1.  **Circle the terms in the box that are used to discuss making steel.**

2.  **Underline the terms that are used to discuss electrical systems.**

| | | |
|---|---|---|
| molds | dynamos | **Bessemer process** |
| converter | blast furnace | fuses          generators |

Use words and phrases from the box to answer the questions below.

3.  **In what did steelworkers melt iron?** _____

4.  **What device held the melted iron as it was turned into steel?**

    _____

5.  **After the melted iron was converted into steel, what was it poured into?**

    _____

6.  **What was one name for the series of steps workers followed in order to**

    **convert iron into steel?** _____

7.  **What are two names for machines that are used to produce electricity?**

    _____

8.  **What did Thomas Edison use to carry electricity from one place to another?**

    _____

Reading and Vocabulary Strategies

Name _____  Date _____

# Inventions Shape Industry

Review pages 499-503 to answer these questions. Choose the best answer. Circle the letter next to your choice.

1. **What was the importance of the Bessemer process?**
   A. Many goods could be made at one time in an assembly line.
   B. Steel could be mass produced at a low cost.
   C. This new art form truly represented America during the Industrial Revolution.
   D. It allowed electricity to provide power for homes all over America.

2. **Before 1770—**
   A. most Americans lived in large cities
   B. steel was cheap and relatively useless
   C. there were no important inventions
   D. most goods were handmade

3. **What was one of the most important uses of steel in the late 1800s?**
   A. making cars
   B. building power lines
   C. building the railroad
   D. making telephones

4. **Who invented the first successful light bulb?**
   A. Joseph Swan
   B. Thomas Edison
   C. Alexander Graham Bell
   D. all of the above

5. **Who was the first person to develop an entire electrical system for a city?**
   A. Thomas Edison
   B. Benjamin Franklin
   C. Henry Bessemer
   D. none of the above

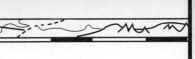

Name _____ Date _____

*Human Systems*

# How Did Geography Help Pittsburgh Grow?

Geography has been important in Pittsburgh's growth. Transportation systems and natural resources helped its steel industry grow. Use this map to answer the questions below.

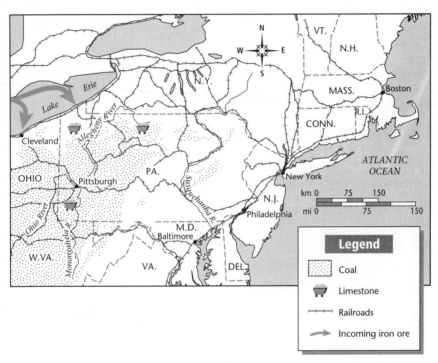

1.  Trace the routes of the three rivers that come together in Pittsburgh in blue.

2.  Mark other major cities situated along railroad routes with a star.

3.  How were Ohio and West Virginia also well positioned for growth? Choose one state. Locate and trace its transportation systems (water and rail). Which natural resources does the state possess?

_____

_____

Think Like a Geographer                    Workbook for Reading and Review    **205**

Name _____   Date _____

# Can You Dig It?

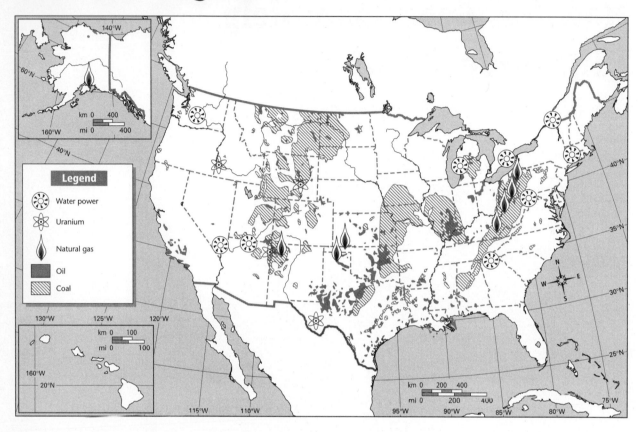

**Legend**

- Water power
- Uranium
- Natural gas
- Oil
- Coal

Use the map above to answer the following questions.

1. **Pittsburgh grew because it is near several important resources. Which energy resources are found near your community? Do they affect the economy of your community? If so, how?**

   _____

   _____

2. **Which resources are found together? Why do you think this happens?**

   _____

   _____

   _____

Name _____ Date _____

Comprehension Skill: Understanding Text Organization—General

# Immigration and Growing Cities

Remember that good writers **organize** information in ways that will help readers understand it.

**1-6.** **The information in your textbook is often organized into main ideas and details. Read the section called "A New Home" on pages 509-510. Supply details from the text that support the two main ideas in the chart below.**

| **Main Idea:** In the late 1800s people left their homelands for many reasons. | **Detail:** |
| | **Detail:** |
| | **Detail:** |

| **Main Idea:** There were also strong factors pulling immigrants to America. | **Detail:** |
| | **Detail:** |
| | **Detail:** |

**7-8.** **Some of the information in this lesson is presented as causes and effects. Read the section called "The Growth of Cities" on pages 510-512. Then complete the cause-and-effect chain below.**

| **Cause:** In American cities, industries and businesses expanded. | → | **Effect/Cause:** |

| **Cause:** Many people, including immigrants, moved to cities to work. | → | **Effect/Cause:** |

Reading and Vocabulary Strategies

Name _____  Date _____

# Immigration and Growing Cities

Review pages 508-512 to answer these questions. Choose the best answer. Circle the letter next to your choice.

1. **Which is an example of an immigrant in the U.S. between 1860 and 1900?**

   A. someone who came from Europe

   B. someone who traveled to the U.S. from Mexico

   C. someone who traveled to the U.S. from Asia

   D. all of the above

2. **What is a *pogrom*?**

   A. an immigrant in the U.S. in the late 1800s

   B. something two cultures have in common

   C. the lowest deck in a cruise ship which carried immigrants

   D. an organized attack on a group of people

3. **Where did most immigrants from Europe arrive?**

   A. at Ellis Island in Richmond, Virginia

   B. at Castle Garden in New York City

   C. at Plymouth Rock in Plymouth, Massachusetts

   D. at San Francisco Bay in California

4. **Where did most immigrants from Asia arrive?**

   A. at Angel Island in San Francisco Bay

   B. at Ellis Island in New York City

   C. at Immigration Station in Atlanta, Georgia

   D. at Portland Center in Portland, Oregon

5. **Why did cities become crowded in the late 1800s?**

   A. because many immigrants settled in cities looking for jobs in factories

   B. because of a drought which sent many farmers looking for work in cities

   C. because the government paid people to move there to build up industries

   D. because there was a possibility of war, and cities were safer

Lesson Review

Name _____ Date _____

Vocabulary Skill: Using a Dictionary

# Workers Organize

Study this diagram of a **dictionary** entry for the word *community*, which appears on page 513 of Lesson 3:

**entry word**
(spelled correctly and divided into syllables)

**pronunciation**
(Use the pronunciation key to help you figure out how to say the word.)

**part of speech**
(usually abbreviated; for example, n. stands for noun)

com•mu•ni•ty (ke myoo ni te) *n.* A group of people who share a common nationality, interests, or characteristics: New York's Puerto Rican community

**definition**
(There may be more than one.)

**example phrase**
(how to use the word)

**1-4.** **Look at the words from Lesson 3 listed below. Use a dictionary to complete the chart. If there is more than one definition listed for a word, write the definition that matches the way the word is used in the lesson. (Hint: You will need to look up the base form of each word.)**

| Word | Pronunciation | Part of speech | Definition |
|------|---------------|----------------|------------|
| **symbolized** (page 513) | | | |
| **requiring** (page 514) | | | |
| **bargained** (page 514) | | | |
| **organize** (page 514) | | | |

Name _____    Date _____

# Workers Organize

Review pages 513-515 to answer these questions. Choose the best answer. Circle the letter next to your choice.

1.  **What happened in Johnstown, Pennsylvania, in 1889?**

    A.  Workers at a cigarmaking factory went on strike, and many people were killed in the violence.

    B.  A dam broke and a great flood killed 2,200 people in a poor section of the city.

    C.  A new steelmaking factory opened, and too many people showed up for jobs.

    D.  Many workers lost their jobs when the railroad there went out of business.

2.  **Why did many urban children begin to work at about the age of 10?**

    A.  to fill the many job openings created by the war

    B.  to learn responsibility needed for adulthood

    C.  to make spending money for candy and toys

    D.  to help support their families

3.  **What is *mechanization*?**

    A.  the production of goods by machines

    B.  the repetition of an action

    C.  the operation of a machine by a worker

    D.  the training of workers to run machines

4.  **What do workers do when they strike?**

    A.  They ask for better pay.

    B.  They refuse to work.

    C.  They refuse to buy the company's product.

    D.  They bargain for better wages.

5.  **What changes came about because of labor unions?**

    A.  better pay

    B.  an eight-hour workday

    C.  safer working conditions

    D.  all of the above

Name _____ Date _____

Comprehension Skill: Understanding an Author's Viewpoint

# Becoming a World Power

An **author's viewpoint** is the way the author feels about a subject. Understanding an author's viewpoint allows you to think critically about what you read.

Reread the introduction to Lesson 4 on page 522. Then answer the questions below with complete sentences.

1. **What kind of person does the author think Queen Liliuokalani was?**

   _____

2. **What clues did you use to figure out the author's viewpoint?**

   _____

   _____

3. **Does the author think Queen Liliuokalani or the sugar and pineapple planters deserved control of Hawaii?**

   _____

4. **What clues helped you figure out the author's viewpoint?**

   _____

   _____

5. **Reread the section called "The Spanish American War" and the "Tell Me More" feature on page 524. Do you think yellow journalism articles about the *Maine* could have affected America's decision to go to war? Explain your answer.**

   _____

   _____

   _____

Reading and Vocabulary Strategies

Name _____ Date _____

# Becoming a World Power

Review pages 522-525 to answer these questions. Choose the best answer. Circle the letter next to your choice.

1. **How did America expand its territory in the late 1800s?**
   A.  by annexing Hawaii and purchasing Alaska from the Russians
   B.  by conquering the Russian army and winning Hawaii and Alaska from Russia
   C.  by signing treaties with the small nations of Hawaii and Alaska
   D.  by purchasing Alaska and Hawaii from European nations

2. **What is one of the most important resources from Alaska today?**
   A.  gold
   B.  oil
   C.  water
   D.  lumber

3. **How did the Spanish-American War help the U.S. to become a world power?**
   A.  It showed France that the U.S. was stronger than they were.
   B.  It gave the U.S. control of two major territories, the Philippines and Puerto Rico.
   C.  It gave the U.S. army control over the world's most important rivers.
   D.  It was fought in Spain, so there was no economic or physical damage to the U.S.

4. **What is *yellow journalism*?**
   A.  reporting old stories on faded, yellowed newsprint
   B.  old newspapers that can tell us about history in the late 1800s
   C.  reporting stories in an exaggerated or untruthful manner
   D.  reporting the news in a positive way with happy endings

5. **Why was the Spanish-American War a very short war?**
   A.  Spain's navy was old and its army was small.
   B.  The U.S. threatened to use atomic weapons.
   C.  Spain didn't know how to combat America's modern weapons.
   D.  An epidemic killed many Spanish soldiers in Cuba.

Lesson Review

Name _____  Date _____

Interpreting Political Cartoons

# Humor with a Point

The political cartoon below is the same one you saw on page 527 of your textbook.
Take a closer look at it. The cartoonist who drew it had a reason for drawing
everything you see.

Write the answers to the following activities after rereading the history of the
Panama Canal on page 526.

1. **Why are there ships huddled about President Roosevelt?**

   _____

2. **What do you think the cartoonist is saying by showing Roosevelt throwing
   a shovel of dirt on the city of Bogota?**

   _____

4. **Who does the small man carrying the flag represent? Why is he so small?**

   _____

Name _____ Date _____

Interpreting Political Cartoons

# What's So Funny?

For this activity, you'll need a newspaper or magazine containing political cartoons. Cut out your favorite one, and then answer these questions.

1. **What is the name and date of your source?**

   _____

2. **What topic in the news is this cartoon related to?**

   _____

   _____

   _____

3. **What message do you think the artist is trying to get across? Why?**

   _____

   _____

   _____

   _____

4. **Which of these styles does the artist use? Mark an X in the matching boxes.**

   ❑ **Symbolism** — *uses pictures to represent objects, events, or relationships*

   ❑ **Caricature** — *an exaggeration of the person or symbol's features*

   ❑ **Satire** — *uses ridicule, humor, or irony to show foolishness or wickedness*

   ❑ **Literary allusion** — *uses well-known quotations from a book or movie*

   ❑ **Pathos** — *stirs feelings of sympathy or compassion; is not meant to be funny*

Skills Workshop

Name _____ Date _____

# An Industrial Society

Review pages 498-529 to answer these questions. Choose the best answer. Circle the letter next to your choice.

1. **Who was Andrew Carnegie?**
   A. the supervisor of the installation of the first power system in New York City
   B. a poor Scottish immigrant who founded a steel company and became very rich
   C. the first person ever to make a telephone call
   D. the inventor of the elevator

2. **How did the nation's entrepreneurs achieve their wealth?**
   A. by starting businesses, then looking for more profitable ways to run them
   B. by finding faster and better ways to handle their office work
   C. by inheriting money from their families
   D. by creating many inventions

3. **What industry attracted many immigrants to Chicago?**
   A. steel making
   B. banking
   C. meatpacking
   D. shoemaking

4. **What was an advantage of living in an ethnic neighborhood?**
   A. Immigrants could easily find foods and goods from many different cultures.
   B. It gave immigrants a place to adjust to their new life.
   C. Immigrants could get to know people who spoke different languages and had different customs.
   D. It had public schools where the children could speak and learn just as they had in their old country.

5. **What was a *settlement house*?**
   A. the first place many immigrants settled before they found permanent homes
   B. a place that provided services for poor residents of a city
   C. a small, crowded apartment where many immigrants lived in a city
   D. a large group of apartments in which people from one culture lived together

Name _____ Date _____

6. **How did industrialization change the lives of workers?**

   A. Many workers lost their jobs because machines took their places.

   B. Workers had to get more education so they could do more highly skilled jobs.

   C. They worked long hours, were paid little, and worked in unsafe conditions.

   D. Many new, interesting jobs were created with the development of machines.

7. **Why did workers form unions in the late 1800s?**

   A. They wanted to learn how to do their work more safely and effectively.

   B. Individual workers felt powerless to change working conditions, so they joined together to bargain with company owners.

   C. Business owners encouraged workers to form groups to improve working conditions.

   D. They decided to work together to persuade the government to give them new jobs.

8. **What was the Great Uprising?**

   A. a flood in Johnstown caused by a broken dam

   B. a protest of angry workers who had lost their jobs in Philadelphia

   C. a strike by the workers at the Carnegie Steel plant in Homestead, Pennsylvania

   D. railroad strikes that sometimes resulted in angry battles between workers and federal troops

9. **Who was Queen Liliuokalani?**

   A. a Hawaiian ruler who fought against the sugar and pineapple planters and lost

   B. the leader of the Philippines who sold her country to the U.S. to get out of debt

   C. a Hawaiian ruler who agreed to join the U.S. for military support

   D. a Philippine queen who visited the U.S. and began a partnership with Roosevelt

10. **Why was Alaska sold to the United States?**

   A. because Britain could no longer manage this settlement so far away

   B. because the Russians had broken a peace treaty with the U.S.

   C. because Canada had no use for this frozen territory

   D. because Russia needed money after being defeated in a war with Britain

Chapter Review

Name _____ Date _____

Vocabulary Skill: Words About a Topic

# The Progressives

Lesson 1 describes problems that many Americans faced in the early twentieth century. Here are words used in the lesson to discuss these problems:

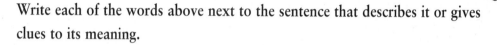

| | | | |
|---|---|---|---|
| unsanitary | Progressives | muckrakers | inspection |
| equal rights | suffragists | factories | |

Write each of the words above next to the sentence that describes it or gives clues to its meaning.

1. **W.E.B. DuBois and the NAACP struggled to get these for African Americans.**

   _____

2. **This is done to make sure that meat is packed under healthy conditions.**

   _____

3. **In the early twentieth century, people who worked to improve many different parts of American society were called by this name.**

   _____

4. **Workers in these places often worked under dangerous conditions.**

   _____

5. **These people struggled to get voting rights for women.**

   _____

6. **Writers who exposed corruption were called this.** _____

7. **This adjective describes the conditions inside many meat-packing plants in the early twentieth century.**

   _____

Name _____  Date _____

# The Progressives

Review pages 535-538 to answer these questions. Choose the best answer. Circle the letter next to your choice.

1.  **What effect did the reading of Upton Sinclair's *The Jungle* have on President Theodore Roosevelt?**
    A.  He read more books by this author.
    B.  He invited Upton Sinclair to the White House.
    C.  He decided to investigate the meat-packing industry.
    D.  He arranged a visit to the African jungle.

2.  **Who were the *Progressives*?**
    A.  a group of government officials who fought for equal rights
    B.  Americans in the early 1900s who wanted to reform business and government
    C.  a group of African Americans who gained the right to vote
    D.  factory owners who didn't want to change working conditions

3.  ***Muckrakers* were people who—**
    A.  didn't have the right to vote
    B.  worked in crowded factories
    C.  worked in meat-packing plants
    D.  searched for and exposed corruption

4.  **What was NOT a problem the Progressives wanted to solve?**
    A.  poor working conditions
    B.  overcrowding on elevators
    C.  long work weeks
    D.  falsely labeled or impure food or drugs

5.  **What made more people pay attention to working conditions in factories?**
    A.  the formation of the NAWSA
    B.  long lines of women and girls who wanted factory jobs
    C.  the fire at the Triangle Shirtwaist Company
    D.  speeches by government officials

Name _____  Date _____

## Comprehension Skill: Making Judgments

# World War I

When you **make a judgment,** you form an opinion about something. Your judgment should be based on facts and logic as well as your own thoughts and beliefs. You can use information from your textbook and your own experiences to make judgments about historical events.

Try making a judgment by answering this question: **"Do you think the United States should have entered World War I?"** First reread the lesson to find out about the United States' entering the war. Then answer the questions below.

1.  **Why were the nations of Europe at war in 1914?**

    _____

2.  **How did President Wilson feel in 1914 about entering the war?**

    _____

3.  **What made President Wilson change his mind?**

    _____

4.  **How did American troops affect the outcome of World War I?**

    _____

5.  **What might have happened if the United States had not entered the war?**

    _____

6.  **Now that you have thought about some facts, make your judgment.**

    I think that the United States (**should/shouldn't**) have entered World War I because:

    _____

    _____

Name _____ Date _____

# World War I

Review pages 539-541 to answer these questions. Choose the best answer. Circle the letter next to your choice.

1. **Which country was part of the Central Powers in World War I?**

    A.  France

    B.  Austria-Hungary

    C.  Britain

    D.  Russia

2. **How did the conditions between 1700 and 1900 bring about war in Europe?**

    A.  Conditions in factories were unsanitary and unsafe.

    B.  Italy was suspicious of France's powerful military.

    C.  European nations had grown steadily, but their growth had led to rivalries.

    D.  The United States had become a world power with overseas territories.

3. **What event began the war?**

    A.  the death of the King of Germany

    B.  the assassination of Archduke Francis Ferdinand

    C.  the overthrow of government buildings in Italy

    D.  the invasion of troops into London

4. **Why did the U.S. enter the war?**

    A.  Germany sank a British passenger ship.

    B.  Tensions increased between the U.S. and Germany.

    C.  Germany attacked unarmed vessels.

    D.  all of the above

5. **What is *trench warfare*?**

    A.  planting bombs in trenches

    B.  attacking major cities of the enemy

    C.  fighting carried out from underground ditches

    D.  fighting near the deep sea trenches

Lesson Review

Name _____ Date _____

*Human Systems*

# Why Did African Americans Move North?

During the Great Migration, African Americans left the rural South in record numbers. They moved north in search of better jobs and better lives.

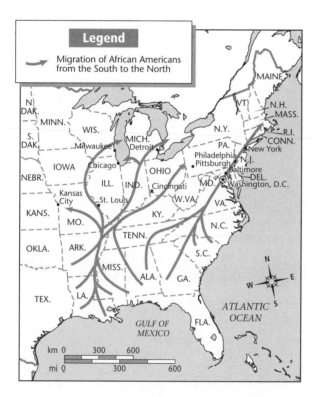

Use the map above to answer the following questions.

1. **To which region did most African Americans from the coastal regions of North and South Carolina and Georgia move?**

    _____

2. **Trace a route from Louisiana to a northern city in blue.**

3. **Why do you think African Americans chose to migrate north instead of west?** _____

    _____

Think Like a Geographer

Name _____ Date _____

# Europe Before World War I

1. **Label the following countries on the map. Use the map on page 541 to help you.**

   **France**    **Germany**
   **Britain**    **Italy**
   **Belgium**    **Russia**
   **Austria-Hungary**

2. **Label all of the countries on the second map.**

3. **Name five countries that came into existence after the war.**

   _____

   _____

   _____

   _____

4. **Why are there now more countries?**

   _____

   _____

   _____

   _____

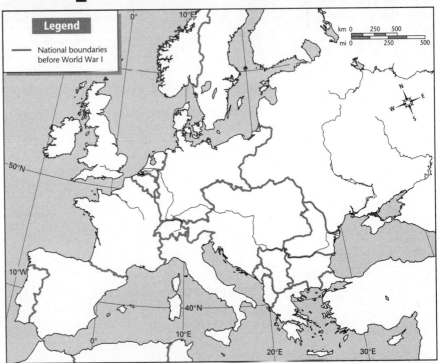

# Europe After World War I

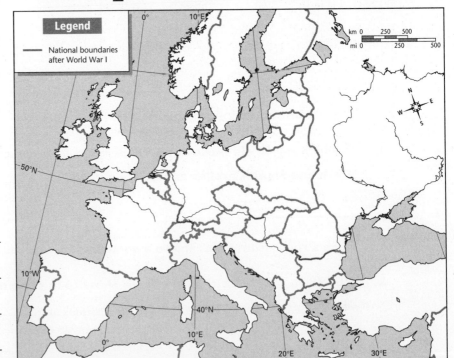

Name _____ Date _____

## Comprehension Strategy: SQ3R

# Good Times, Bad Times

Take some time to review the steps of the **SQ3R** strategy:

**S:** **Survey** the lesson or chapter. Read the main headings and
subheadings. Look at the visuals and read the captions.

**Q:** Make each heading or subheading into a **question.**

**R:** **Read** the lesson to find the answers to those questions.

**R:** **Recite** (say aloud) and **write** the answers to your questions.

**R:** **Review** the lesson by rereading your questions and answers.

Follow the steps of SQ3R for Lesson 3. Before you read the lesson, complete
Column One. After you read the lesson, complete Column Two.

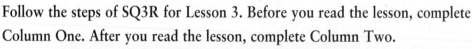

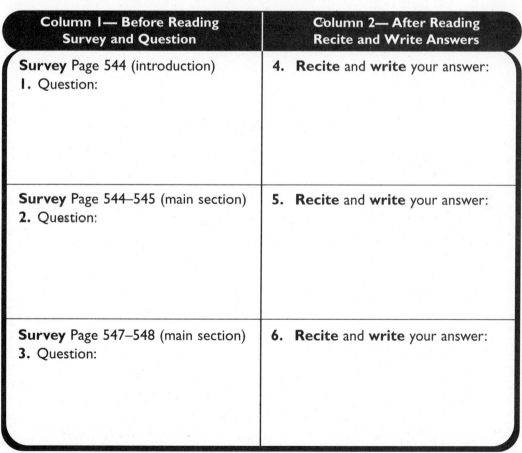

| Column I— Before Reading Survey and Question | Column 2— After Reading Recite and Write Answers |
|---|---|
| **Survey** Page 544 (introduction) <br> I. Question: | **4. Recite** and **write** your answer: |
| **Survey** Page 544–545 (main section) <br> 2. Question: | **5. Recite** and **write** your answer: |
| **Survey** Page 547–548 (main section) <br> 3. Question: | **6. Recite** and **write** your answer: |

**7.** **Finally, review the lesson by rereading the information you recorded in
your chart.**

Reading and Vocabulary Strategies

Name _____    Date _____

# Good Times, Bad Times

Review pages 544-548 to answer these questions. Choose the best answer. Circle the letter next to your choice.

1.  **Which is NOT a change that took place in the U.S. in the 1920s?**

    A.  More women joined the workforce.

    B.  New York City became a center of great artistic activity.

    C.  The nation's economy grew and prospered.

    D.  Radios and televisions became popular forms of entertainment.

2.  **What is another name for African Americans' creative achievement in the 1920s?**

    A.  the Civilian Conservation Corps

    B.  the New Deal

    C.  the Roaring Twenties

    D.  the Harlem Renaissance

3.  **What is the *stock market*?**

    A.  a place where products can be made quickly, cheaply, and in large numbers

    B.  a place where products from all over the world are sold

    C.  a place where fish are sold to be stocked in lakes

    D.  a place where people buy and sell shares of stock in companies

4.  **What happened on "Black Tuesday"?**

    A.  The prices of stock fell so fast that day that it was called a "crash."

    B.  A terrible epidemic began to spread in New York City.

    C.  The U.S. became involved in World War II.

    D.  Roosevelt announced that, "The only thing we have to fear is fear itself."

5.  **What is a *depression*?**

    A.  a severe business slowdown

    B.  the lowering of prices

    C.  the failure of a business

    D.  the production of too many goods

Lesson Review

Name _____ Date _____

Predicting Outcomes Using Graphs

# Predicting the Future

Study these two line graphs about the Great Depression. One shows the number of houses or apartment buildings started in a year. The other shows the number of people who were unemployed.

1. **In which year were the most buildings (units) begun?**

   _____

2. **In the years between 1928 and 1933, what happened to the number of housing units begun?**

   _____

3. **In what year were the largest number of people out of work?**

   _____

4. **Predict what might have happened in 1936 for each graph. Explain your answer.**

   _____

   _____

   _____

   _____

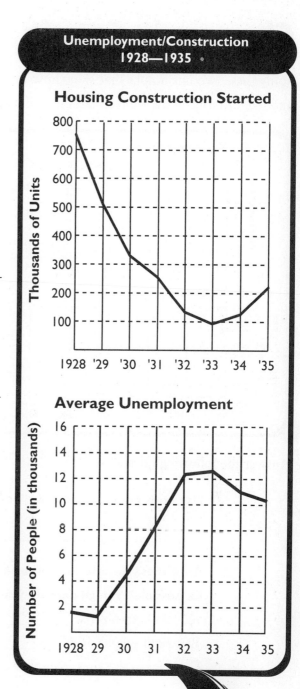

**Unemployment/Construction 1928—1935**

**Housing Construction Started**

Thousands of Units

1928 '29 '30 '31 '32 '33 '34 '35

**Average Unemployment**

Number of People (in thousands)

1928 29 30 31 32 33 34 35

Name _____  Date _____

Predicting Outcomes Using Graphs

# Changes in Farming

Study these two line graphs that show how the number
and size of farms in the United States has changed.

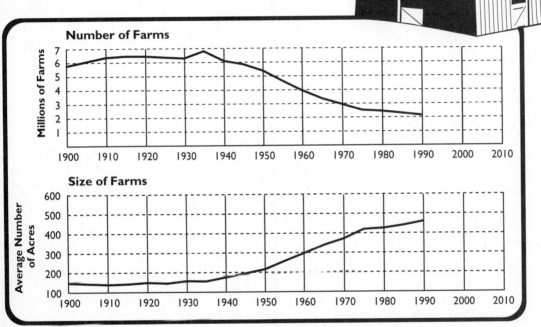

**Number of Farms**

Millions of Farms

**Size of Farms**

Average Number of Acres

Answer the following questions.

1. **Use both graphs to describe how farms changed in the 20th century.**

   _____

2. **Read these descriptions of future trends. Which ones do you think might
   be possible? Which ones do you think wouldn't occur? Why.**

   A. Both graphs rise. _____

   B. Both graphs drop. _____

   C. One graph rises, the other drops. _____

3. **What do you predict will happen in the future to the number and size of
   farms? Plot your predictions for the years 2000 and 2010 on the graphs.**

   _____

   _____

Name _____  Date _____

## Comprehension Skill: Understanding Sequence of Events

# World War II

Remember that **sequence** is the order in which events happen.

On page 550, read the introduction to Lesson 4 and the first paragraph of the section called "Mobilizing for War." Then answer the questions below.

1. **Which event is described in the first two paragraphs on 550?**

   _____

2. **Which events are described in the third paragraph on page 550?**

   _____

3. **In what order did the events described in these three paragraphs happen?**

   _____

4. **Review Lesson 4. Then write a number on the line in front of each sentence to show the correct order of these events.**

   _____ Japan attacked the United States naval base at Pearl Harbor.

   _____ Japan surrendered to the United States.

   _____ Germany and Italy went to war with the Allied Powers.

   _____ Japan joined the Axis Powers.

   _____ D-Day: The Allies invaded Normandy, France.

   _____ Germany and Italy declared war on the United States.

   _____ Hitler formed an alliance between Germany and Italy.

   _____ The United States Congress declared war on Japan.

   _____ The United States dropped atomic bombs on Hiroshima and Nagasaki.

   _____ Germany surrendered to the Allies.

Name _____ Date _____

# World War II

Review pages 550-555 to answer these questions. Choose the best answer. Circle the letter next to your choice.

I. **How did World War II begin?**

   A. Germany refused to pay money to the Allies after World War I.

   B. Germany went to war against the Allies in 1939.

   C. Hitler declared war on France in 1937.

   D. Britain declared war on Germany in 1938.

2. **Who were members of the Allied Powers in World War II?**

   A. Britain, Poland, France, the United States

   B. Poland, Italy, Algeria, Japan, Vietnam

   C. France, Britain, Italy, Germany

   D. Austria, the United States, Switzerland, Mexico

3. **What was the *Holocaust*?**

   A. a mass murder of Jews and other minorities by the Nazis

   B. another name for the attack on Pearl Harbor

   C. a kind of prison where Japanese Americans were forced to live

   D. total destruction of the country of Italy

4. **What was *D-Day*?**

   A. the dropping of the atomic bomb on Hiroshima

   B. the day that President Eisenhower announced the end of World War II

   C. the Allies' invasion of Normandy, France

   D. the day that the Great Depression ended

5. **What is an *atomic bomb*?**

   A. a new kind of weapon that could be used on submarines

   B. a bomb using nuclear energy

   C. a weapon using poisonous grenades

   D. a bomb developed during World War II that was never used

Name _____ Date _____

# A New World Power

Review pages 534-557 to answer these questions. Choose the best answer. Circle the letter next to your choice.

1. **Why was the 19th Amendment important?**
   A. It gave women the right to vote in all elections.
   B. It freed all enslaved people.
   C. It required that meat be packed under sanitary conditions.
   D. It improved working conditions in factories.

2. **What did African Americans accomplish during the Progressive Era?**
   A. the establishment of the NAACP and the continued struggle for equal rights
   B. the right to live wherever they chose
   C. equal opportunities for employment
   D. the establishment of colleges for African American students

3. **What is an *armistice*?**
   A. an end to fighting
   B. a military advantage
   C. a kind of bomb
   D. a tool used to dig a trench

4. **America signed a peace treaty with—**
   A. Italy
   B. the League of Nations
   C. Germany
   D. Austria-Hungary

5. **Who was Charles Lindbergh?**
   A. the designer of short dresses for the flappers
   B. an African American writer who lived in New York City
   C. the first person to fly alone, nonstop, across the Atlantic
   D. the creator of the assembly line

Name _____ Date _____

6. **How did the Great Depression affect American life?**

   A. The entertainment industry almost closed down completely.

   B. Women began to volunteer, since most of them had lost their jobs.

   C. Millions of Americans lost their jobs, their homes, and their confidence.

   D. Many immigrants returned to their home countries to look for work.

7. **What did President Roosevelt's New Deal do?**

   A. It put factory workers on the job day and night to build weapons needed in World War II.

   B. It started federal work programs and passed laws to help individuals who could not work.

   C. It encouraged grandparents to become volunteers and help those who were needy.

   D. It helped bring back the good times of the 1920s.

8. *Social Security* **is a program that—**

   A. gives jobs to people who are unemployed

   B. employs young workers for public projects, such as maintaining parks

   C. provides insurance for the unemployed and support money for senior citizens

   D. rebuilds roads, buildings, bridges, and airports

9. **Why did the United States join the Allies?**

   A. to "settle the score" from the last war with Germany

   B. to take North Africa from the Axis Powers

   C. because the Japanese had attacked Pearl Harbor

   D. because Hitler threatened to attack New York

10. **What did the** *D* **stand for in** *D-Day?*

    A. destruction

    B. the secret date of a planned military operation

    C. Dwight D. Eisenhower

    D. Depression

Chapter Review

Name _____  Date _____

## Vocabulary Skill: Greek and Latin Roots

# Life in the 1950s

Many English words have Greek and Latin **roots**. The charts below show some Greek and Latin roots, what their meanings are, and examples of words that come from them.

| Greek Root | Meaning | English word |
|---|---|---|
| *hydro* | "water" | *hydroelectricity* ("electricity generated by water") |
| *demos* | "people" | *demography* ("the study of the traits of a group of people") |
| *komos* | "noisy celebration" | *comedy* ("a funny play or movie") |

| Latin Root | Meaning | English word |
|---|---|---|
| *super* | "over, above" | *superior* ("higher or better than someone or something else") |
| *dividere* | "to divide" | *divisible* ("able to be divided") |
| *optimus* | "best" | *optimize* ("to make the best of") |

The words below appear in Lesson 1. Circle the root in each word. Using the meaning of the root plus the context in which the word appears, write a definition for each word. Finally, check your definitions in a dictionary.

1. **democracy** (page 560) _____

2. **optimism** (page 562) _____

3. **comedienne** (page 562) _____

4. **hydrogen** (page 559) _____

5. **superpowers** (page 561) _____

6. **division** (page 560) _____

Name _____   Date _____

# Life in the 1950s

Review pages 559-562 to answer these questions. Choose the best answer. Circle the letter next to your choice.

1. **Why were Americans afraid of nuclear attack in the 1950s?**
   A. because World War II was taking place in Europe
   B. because the Vietnam War was taking place
   C. because there was a race between the U.S. and the Soviet Union to develop powerful bombs
   D. because America was in a nuclear war with Germany

2. **What is *communism*?**
   A. a government in which the power is held by elected officials
   B. a system in which all schools are run by the students
   C. a system in which the government owns businesses
   D. a government controlled by the nobility

3. **What was the *Iron Curtain*?**
   A. a metal wall separating Communist and non-Communist countries
   B. a wall that separated East and West Germany
   C. a machine used to help people with breathing problems
   D. a line dividing democratic and Communist countries in Europe

4. **The *Cold War* was a war—**
   A. in which no weapons were used
   B. fought in Alaska
   C. fought in the cold regions of the Soviet Union
   D. that used powerful bombs

5. **What was life like for families that moved to the suburbs in the 1950s?**
   A. not much extra money for food, shelter, and clothing
   B. going to the movies, listening to radio shows, and playing computer games
   C. having babies, buying consumer goods, and watching television
   D. many single-parent families and large, extended families with grandparents living in the same house

Name _____ Date _____

## Comprehension Skill: Analyzing Bias

# Civil Rights Movement

A **bias** is a strong opinion for or against something. When many people share the same bias, it can result in customs that favor of one group over another.

Answer the questions below with complete sentences.

1. **Read the section called "Segregation" on pages 563–564. What were some of the laws that supported segregation in the United States?**

   _____

   _____

   _____

2. **Read the section called "Protest" on pages 564-567. What did people do to change segregation laws?**

   _____

   _____

   _____

**Assumptions** are ideas that are accepted as true without proof. It is important to identify assumptions so you can decide whether they are truthful or not.

3. **Read these statements. Decide which are assumptions and circle them.**
   A. Nonviolent protest will lead to social change.
   B. Rosa Parks was arrested for refusing to give her seat to a white person on a bus.
   C. You can't fight prejudice because people will never change.
   D. "Sit-ins" at lunch counters were held in 54 cities in nine states.

Name _____     Date _____

# Civil Rights Movement

Review pages 563-567 to answer these questions. Choose the best answer. Circle the letter next to your choice.

1. **Who was Rosa Parks?**

   A. a young African American minister who fought for civil rights

   B. the first African American woman lawyer

   C. a founder of one of the first African American colleges

   D. an African American arrested for refusing to give her bus seat to a white man

2. **What are *civil rights*?**

   A. rights of businesses to serve whomever they chose

   B. fair and equal treatment under the Constitution

   C. opportunities to work for freedom

   D. protests against segregation

3. **How did segregation affect African Americans?**

   A. It barred them from certain places.

   B. It kept them from voting.

   C. It limited their educational, economic, and social opportunities.

   D. all of the above

4. **How did African Americans gain rights for themselves?**

   A. with boycotts, sit-ins, and marches through the South

   B. by becoming news reporters and telling their stories

   C. by abstaining from voting in presidential elections

   D. all of the above

5. **In what year did the Civil Rights Act make segregation illegal in all 50 states?**

   A. 1964

   B. 1960

   C. 1969

   D. 1972

Lesson Review

Name _____ Date _____

Comprehension Skill: Understanding Text Organization–Special Features

# The War in Vietnam

Your textbook has **special features** that give more information about the topics in the lessons. Understanding how a special feature is organized helps you understand the information in it.

Study the diagram on page 573. Read the captions. Then answer the questions below.

1.  **What does the diagram show?**

    _____

2.  **How do the lines from the captions to the illustration help readers?**

    _____

3.  **What does the photograph just above the diagram show?**

    _____

4.  **Why did the Huey need a large, powerful engine?**

    _____

Study the timeline on page 574 and read the caption. Then answer the questions.

5.  **What information about the Vietnam War does the timeline show?**

    _____

    _____

6.  **How does looking at the timeline help you understand important information about the Vietnam War? Explain your answer.**

    _____

    _____

    _____

Reading and Vocabulary Strategies

Name _____ Date _____

# The War in Vietnam

Review pages 572-575 to answer these questions. Choose the best answer. Circle the letter next to your choice.

1. **What are *developing nations*?**
   A. countries where there is not enough food, resources, and money for the people who live there
   B. nations that are developing many weapons
   C. countries that are growing rapidly because of the numbers of people immigrating there
   D. nations in which Communist governments control all aspects of life

2. **Why did America join forces with South Vietnam?**
   A. to keep a civil war from starting in Vietnam
   B. to keep communism from spreading
   C. to force Germany out of Vietnam
   D. to help South Vietnam fight for its independence from Korea

3. **What was the main difference for most Americans between the Vietnam War and other U.S. wars?**
   A. This was the first time newspaper reporters took photographs of a war.
   B. People could watch images of the war on television.
   C. This war was fought in the air.
   D. American forces lost most major battles of the war.

4. **What was the American public's reaction to the Vietnam War?**
   A. Many protested and demanded that U.S. troops pull out of the conflict.
   B. Some supported U.S. involvement in the war.
   C. Some said the U.S. should not be fighting in another country's civil war.
   D. all of the above

5. **How did many young Americans feel when the war was over?**
   A. that the U.S. had done the right thing by fighting this war
   B. that they would go to war again to help spread democracy in the world
   C. glad that Vietnam's civil war was over and there was peace once more
   D. that the U.S. had lost its way, and they blamed it on American culture

Lesson Review

Name _____ Date _____

Comprehension Skill: Recognizing Fact and Opinion

# A World of Change

A **fact** is a statement that can be proven. An **opinion** is a statement that tells how a person thinks or feels and cannot be proven. Here are two examples:

| | |
|---|---|
| **Fact:** *Patsy Takemoto Mink was elected to Congress in 1964.* | **Opinion:** *Women should get "equal pay for equal work."* |

1. **Review the introduction to Lesson 4 on page 578. What opinion about people with disabilities probably led to the passing of the ADA? Circle the letter next to that opinion.**

   A. People with disabilities should be able to enter stores and public offices.

   B. People with disabilities should use separate facilities.

Answer the questions below.

2. **Review the first three paragraphs of the section called "Struggle for Equality" on page 579. What was Cesar Chávez's opinion about the treatment of California grape pickers during the 1960s?**

   _____

3. **Review the section called "Native Americans' Rights" on pages 579-580. In the opinion of AIM members, what were the government's responsibilities to Native Americans?**

   _____

   _____

Name _____ Date _____

# A World of Change

Review pages 578-582 to answer these questions. Choose the best answer. Circle the letter next to your choice.

1. **The American Disabilities Act of 1990—**
   A. protects the rights of disabled people to enter schools and other buildings
   B. provides special employment opportunities for disabled persons
   C. funds companies to design special vehicles for disabled people
   D. allows all disabled adults to get driver's licenses

2. **Who is a *migrant worker*?**
   A. a person who manages a farm
   B. a person who moves from place to place looking for farm work
   C. someone who helps Mexican Americans begin their own farms
   D. one who lives and works on a farm all year long

3. **What rights have Native Americans gained in the past three decades?**
   A. Native American colleges and universities have been established.
   B. Native Americans got some of their land back and the right to run health, education, and housing programs.
   C. Native Americans have special organizations to fight against crime.
   D. Native Americans have the right to take back land from the government.

4. **What rights have women gained in the past three decades?**
   A. the right to become President
   B. the right to vote
   C. improved economic and political opportunities
   D. all of the above

5. **What did the end of the Cold War mean for Americans?**
   A. an end to high prices for fuel
   B. no need to spend money for military improvements
   C. an end to the arms race and more cooperation between the U.S. and the Soviet Union
   D. increased the educational opportunities throughout the world

Lesson Review

Name _____     Date _____

## Producing Oral Histories

# Talking History

Use this page to plan an interview that you will use to create an oral history.

1. **What is your topic?** _____

2. **What key facts do you already know about your topic?**

   _____

   _____

   _____

3. **Whom did you choose to interview for your oral history? Why?**

   _____

   _____

4. **What are four questions you want to ask your interviewee?**

   _____

   _____

   _____

   _____

Interview

1. Topic: _____

2. Name of Person: _____

3. Questions: _____

Skills Workshop

Name _____     Date _____

Producing Oral Histories

# Think About It

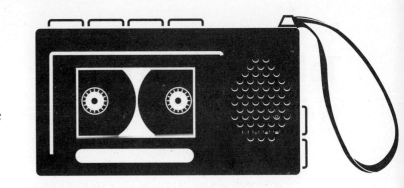

Prepare to record an interview with someone who lived during the 1950s to create an oral history. Use this page as a follow up.

**1. Whom would you interview?**

_____

**2. What are three questions you would ask?**

**Question 1:** _____

_____

**Question 2:** _____

_____

**Question 3:** _____

_____

**3. What would you do differently if you wanted to learn about the Vietnam War? Why?**

_____

_____

_____

**4. For the next history topic you study, do you want to create an oral history as part of your research? Why or why not?**

_____

_____

Name _____  Date _____

# Into the 21st Century

Review pages 558-58 to answer these questions. Choose the best answer. Circle the letter next to your choice.

1. **What is *capitalism*?**

    A.  government by election

    B.  free enterprise, or ownership by the people

    C.  an economic system of a representative democracy

    D.  a settlement ruled by a distant country

2. **What is *nonviolent protest*?**

    A.  a movement by government officials to demand that protestors act peacefully

    B.  a quiet way to show the government that it is powerful

    C.  trying to change unfair laws by refusing to obey them

    D.  writing letters to the editor to tell how someone feels

3. **The *Freedom Riders* were young people who—**

    A.  went south by bus from Washington, D.C., and used whites-only restrooms and waiting rooms in the bus stations

    B.  rode horses up and down Pennsylvania Avenue demanding equal rights

    C.  joined Martin Luther King, Jr., to march against segregation

    D.  rode bicycles through the South to protest against segregation

4. **How did segregation end in Birmingham, Alabama?**

    A.  Dr. King joined with Rosa Parks and others to stop riding the buses.

    B.  Pictures taken of African American protestors being treated cruelly by police shocked many Americans and led to changes.

    C.  Students refused to attend classes until the governor would discuss civil rights.

    D.  An African American doctor saved the life of a Birmingham government official.

5. **What effect did the Vietnam War have on Americans?**

    A.  It split America on the issue of whether or not U.S. troops should be there.

    B.  Many Americans became volunteers to help the war efforts in Vietnam.

    C.  It caused many violent protests and strikes.

    D.  It united Americans because they wanted Vietnam to be a democracy.

Name _____    Date _____

6. **What was the outcome of the Vietnam War?**

   A. South Vietnam defeated North Vietnam.

   B. Vietnam won its independence from Korea.

   C. The U.S. pulled out of Vietnam, and North Vietnam conquered South Vietnam.

   D. German forces pulled out of South Vietnam.

7. **Which President brought all the U.S. troops home from Vietnam?**

   A. John F. Kennedy

   B. Richard Nixon

   C. George Bush

   D. Gerald Ford

8. **What rights have Mexican Americans gained in the past three decades?**

   A. Mexican American migrant workers have a labor union and are treated more fairly.

   B. Mexican American colleges and universities have been established.

   C. Mexican Americans have the right to move their families to America for free.

   D. Mexican Americans have the right to vote in both Mexico and the U.S.

9. **What happened at Wounded Knee, South Dakota, in 1973?**

   A. Two hundred Native Americans took over the village until the government promised to consider their demands.

   B. There was a battle between Native Americans and the U.S. government that ended with the release of people unfairly put in jail.

   C. The American Indian Movement was established to fight for Native Americans' civil rights.

   D. The Bureau of Indian Affairs agreed to protect Native Americans against crime and discrimination.

10. **What did Mikhail Gorbachev achieve?**

    A. He agreed to work with President Clinton to have joint space missions.

    B. He urged all Russians and Americans to "ask not what your country can do for you . . . Ask what you can do for your country."

    C. He ended the era of kings and queens in the former Soviet Union.

    D. He opened the former Soviet Union and Eastern Europe to democracy.

Name _____     Date _____

Comprehension Strategy: Previewing a Lesson

# Canada

When you **preview** a lesson or chapter, you look ahead at the information in it to find out what you will learn.

Look at the Chapter Preview at the bottom of pages 588-589. Read the titles and captions that come with the photos. Then answer these questions:

1.   **What are two countries you will read about in Chapter 22?**

   _____

   _____

2.   **What Mexican city will you read about in Chapter 22?**

   _____

Look through Lesson 1. Read the title, the Main Idea sentence, the headings, and the Focus questions. Write the headings here:

3.   **page 590:** _____

4.   **page 592:** _____

Now look at the chart, the map, and the other visuals in Lesson 1. Describe what each visual shows. One has been described for you.

5.   **page 590:** _____

6.   **page 591:** _____

7.   **page 592:** _____

8.   **page 593:** _a photo of Montreal and a sign that says "Great Divide" in both English and French_

Name _____ Date _____

# Canada

Review pages 589-593 to answer these questions. Choose the best answer. Circle the letter next to your choice.

1. **What is the _Canadian Shield_?**

   A. the name of the nation's health insurance plan

   B. the group of mounted police that patrols the Canadian border

   C. a rock formation that covers much of eastern Canada

   D. a mountain that protects the southern half of Canada from bitter cold winds

2. **What is a _province_?**

   A. an area with its own government, much like a U.S. state

   B. a water route to markets in the United States and around the world

   C. the leader of a government group that makes the laws in Canada

   D. a trade agreement between Canada and the United States

3. **Where do most Canadians live?**

   A. in the north in Victoria and Baffin

   B. in the west in Vancouver and Calgary

   C. in the southeast in Quebec and Ontario

   D. in central Canada in and around Winnipeg

4. **How does the St. Lawrence Seaway help Canada trade with other nations?**

   A. by providing a water route to markets around the world

   B. by giving people an affordable way to travel to other nations

   C. all the cities of Canada are on this waterway

   D. by connecting the Great Lakes to the Pacific Ocean

5. **What does _bilingual_ mean?**

   A. having two or more homes

   B. speaking two languages or having two official languages

   C. a culture influenced by a mix of many other cultures

   D. speaking three or more languages

Name _____ Date _____

## Comprehension Skill: Drawing Conclusions

# Mexico

You have learned to **draw conclusions** about topics in your textbook by combining facts from the text with your own knowledge.

Reread the feature called "Curious Facts" on page 597. The chart below shows how to draw a conclusion based on information from that feature.

| Facts from the text | | Your own knowledge | | Conclusion |
|---|---|---|---|---|
| *Workers uncovered an Aztec pyramid while digging in Mexico City.* | **+** | *When a civilization dies out, traces of its existence may remain for a long time.* | **=** | *Aztecs once lived where Mexico City is located today.* |

Now reread the captions of the map feature on page 595. Use the chart below to draw a conclusion to answer the Map Skill question: "Do you think it is difficult to build highways and railroads across Mexico?"

| Facts from the text | | Your own knowledge | | Conclusion |
|---|---|---|---|---|
| | **+** | | **=** | |

Workbook for Reading and Review **245**

Name _____ Date _____

# Mexico

Review pages 594-598 to answer these questions. Choose the best answer. Circle the letter next to your choice.

1. **Which is NOT a geographic region of Mexico?**

   A. Central Plateau

   B. Baja California

   C. Rocky Mountains

   D. Yucatan Peninsula

2. **How are Mexicans shaping their future?**

   A. by improving trade with foreign nations and by providing more jobs

   B. by working with Spain to improve their economy

   C. by learning European methods of education and farming

   D. by encouraging more workers to move to Mexico City

3. **What does _infrastructure_ mean?**

   A. a country's system of transportation and communication

   B. the way a country's government is structured

   C. the amount of money the government spends on public assistance

   D. the improvement of education, housing, and medical care

4. **What groups make up the blend of cultures in modern Mexico?**

   A. Canadian and Californian cultures

   B. Spanish and Native American cultures

   C. French and Italian cultures

   D. North American and South American cultures

5. **How can education help solve the employment problem in Mexico?**

   A. by training people to be teachers

   B. by teaching people many different languages to communicate across the world

   C. by training people for jobs in modern industries

   D. by teaching people how to apply for jobs

Lesson Review

Name _____ Date _____

Vocabulary Skill: Key Vocabulary

# Nations Working Together

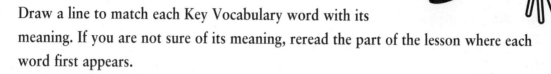

The **Key Vocabulary** terms for Lesson 3 are *trading partner*, *tariff*, *NAFTA*, and *grassroots*. Knowing these words will help you understand and remember the information in this lesson.

Draw a line to match each Key Vocabulary word with its meaning. If you are not sure of its meaning, reread the part of the lesson where each word first appears.

1.   **trading partners**

A.   a treaty that will make it easier for the United States, Canada, and Mexico to trade with each other

2.   **tariff**

B.   groups of ordinary citizens working for a common goal

3.   **NAFTA**

C.   countries that sell many goods to each other

4.   **grassroots groups**

D.   an extra tax on goods brought into a country

Answer the following questions with complete sentences.

5.   **Do tariffs encourage or discourage trade between nations? Why?**

_____

6.   **What do the letters NAFTA stand for?** _____

_____

7.   **According to some critics, how might NAFTA harm people in the United States?** _____

_____

8.   **What is one way NAFTA may benefit people in the United States?**

_____

Name _____ Date _____

# Nations Working Together

Review pages 599-603 to answer these questions. Choose the best answer. Circle the letter next to your choice.

1.  **How has increased trade affected the nations of the Americas?**
    A.  There is less competition, and it has forced prices of goods down.
    B.  Additional tariffs have made imports cost less.
    C.  Disagreements between nations have increased, sometimes causing violence.
    D.  People have more products to choose from, and trade helps nations grow.

2.  **What is a *trading partner*?**
    A.  a state that trades with another state without charging taxes
    B.  a business that locates its industry in many nations
    C.  a country that frequently trades goods with another country
    D.  a company that helps similar businesses in another nation

3.  **What is a *tariff*?**
    A.  a stamp with the date an item was imported
    B.  a tax on goods brought into a country
    C.  a translation of a label written in another language
    D.  all of the above

4.  **Why is Simón Bolívar called "the George Washington of South America"?**
    A.  He led South American nations to independence from Spain.
    B.  He hoped that all American nations would someday work together.
    C.  He was the first President of South America.
    D.  He often wore a three-cornered hat like George Washington.

5.  **What does *grassroots* mean?**
    A.  ordinary citizens working toward a common goal
    B.  people who come from farming communities to work together
    C.  crops, like grains, which can feed many people
    D.  a campaign against political injustice

Lesson Review

Name _____ Date _____

Interpreting Map Perspectives

# Right Side Up, Upside Down

Study this view of North America. Compare it to the maps on pages 604–605 in your textbook.

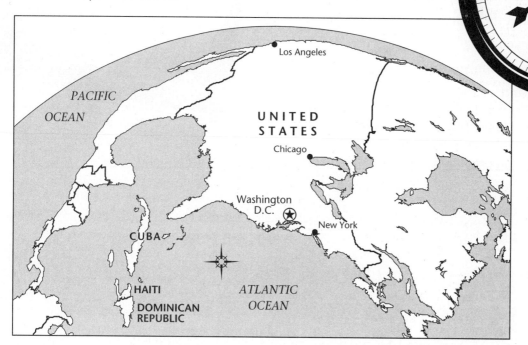

1. **Find the United States. Where is Mexico? Where is Canada? Label all three countries.**

2. **On most maps, North is "up." Where is North on this map? Finish the compass rose for this map by labeling the directions N, S, E, and W.**

3. **Is the area of the country where you live shown on this map? If yes, mark an X at its location and explain how you found it. If not, explain how the map would need to change to include your location.**

_____

_____

_____

_____

Name _____ Date _____

## Interpreting Map Perspectives

# Where Are You?

Do you recognize these states? Imagine you are the little person below each state, then answer the following questions. (Look at the sample answer before you begin.)

- where you are
- what direction you are looking
- what state you see

Use a map of the United States to help you.

**Sample Answer:** *I am standing in the Atlantic Ocean, looking west at Florida.*

1. 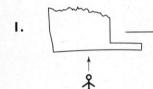 _____

2. 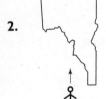 _____

3. _____

4. _____

Name _____ Date _____

# A Hemisphere of Neighbors

Review pages 588-607 to answer these questions. Choose the best answer. Circle the letter next to your choice.

1. **What resources does Canada have that are in short supply in the world today?**
   A. coal and sulfur
   B. trees, petroleum, and good farmland
   C. clean air, land, and water
   D. salt and spices

2. **What kind of society have Canadians built?**
   A. a society that is strongly tied to Spanish and Native American cultures
   B. a society where people are more alike than different in culture
   C. a unique society in which many people speak French, English, and Spanish
   D. a bilingual, multicultural society with strong British and French roots

3. **What is a *French-Canadian separatist*?**
   A. someone who speaks only the French-Canadian language
   B. one who was born in France and moved to Canada
   C. one who would like Canada to end trade with France
   D. a person who would like Quebec to become an independent nation

4. **Which of the following resources have contributed to Mexico's economy?**
   A. gold and silver
   B. oil and crops
   C. coal and zinc
   D. all of the above

5. **What surrounds Mexico City?**
   A. rivers
   B. mountains
   C. oceans
   D. volcanoes

6. **What is a *standard of living*?**

   A. the kind of entertainment that people like

   B. the type of job held by most people in a community

   C. the way a government uses its money to make the economy grow

   D. the amount of money people spend on themselves and their families

7. **Why do governments place tariffs on imported goods?**

   A. to let people know about expiration dates

   B. to inform consumers about warnings associated with the product

   C. to help the country in which the product was made

   D. to encourage people to buy goods manufactured or grown in their own country

8. **What does NAFTA do?**

   A. controls the number of foreign workers coming into countries

   B. decides where countries can locate foreign factories

   C. makes it easier for countries to trade with each other

   D. works on improving education and health services among countries

9. **What is the OAS?**

   A. Order of American Safety

   B. Organization of American States

   C. Obligation of American Society

   D. Our American Surroundings

10. **What is the purpose of the OAS?**

   A. to protect the environment and increase trade between American nations

   B. to protect each other from high taxes and economic disaster

   C. to provide mutual safety and protection for all American nations

   D. to help each other improve roads, buildings, and communication systems